SURVIVAL
MANUAL

BONSAI SURVIVAL MANUAL

*Tree-by-tree guide to buying,
maintaining, and problem solving*

COLIN LEWIS

A *Storey Publishing* Book

STOREY

Storey Communications, Inc.
Pownal, VT 05261

635.9172
Low

Copyright © 1996 Quarto Inc

United States edition published in 1996 by Storey Communications, Inc., Schoolhouse Road, Pownal, Vermont 05261.

The mission of Storey Communications is to serve our customers by publishing practical information that encourages personal independence in harmony with the environment.

This book was designed and produced by
Quarto Publishing plc
The Old Brewery
6 Blundell Street
London N7 9BH

Senior editors Sian Parkhouse, Louisa McDonnell
Copy editor Chester Krone
Senior art editor Catherine Shearman
Illustrator Ann Savage
Designer Anne Fisher
Photographer Ian Howes
Picture research Miriam Hyman
Picture manager Giulia Hetherington
Editorial director Mark Dartford
Art director Moira Clinch
Storey Communications editor Gwen W. Steege

Typeset in Great Britain by Central Southern Typesetters
Manufactured in Hong Kong by Regent Publishing Services Ltd
Printed in China by Leefung Asco Printers Ltd

10 9 8 7 6 5 4 3 2 1

Library of Congress Cataloging-in-Publication Data

Lewis, Colin. 1948–
    Bonsai survival manual : Tree-by-tree guide to buying,
    maintaining, and problem solving /
Colin Lewis.
        p.   cm.
    Includes index.
    ISBN 0-88266-853-6 (pb : alk. paper)
        Bonsai.   I. Title
SB433.5.L475   1996   96-1718
635.9'772–dc20   CIP

CONTENTS

FOREWORD   6

INTRODUCTION   8

CHAPTER ONE
BUYING BONSAI   12

CHAPTER TWO
CARING FOR YOUR BONSAI   20

CHAPTER THREE
SHAPING YOUR BONSAI   32

CHAPTER FOUR
PESTS AND DISEASES   48

SPECIES PROFILES   56

LIST OF SUPPLIERS   158

INDEX   159

CREDITS   160

FOREWORD

BONSAI COMBINES THE beauty of manmade sculpture with the harmony and perfection of nature in one art form. All parts of a bonsai – roots, trunk, branches, foliage, and container – must, like traditional sculpture, express the artist's feeling for balance, form, and line. But when these are combined with the life forces of the natural world, they evoke a larger and deeper concept. A bonsai is a microcosm containing within it, unchanged in everything but size, the mystery of the universe. Bonsai artists may encourage the bonsai to express itself, they may assist and aid it, but they always respect the essence of the tree.

Bonsai are ordinary living trees which have been miniaturized by sound horticultural techniques. In the process, they have been shaped by the artist so that, in their entirety, they express the beauty of a tree growing in a natural environment. To capture the essence of a tree is to bring nature home. Watching a maple tree – small enough to hold in your hands – sprout its tiny buds in the spring, fill out with its deep green foliage in the summer, turn bright red in the fall, and drop its leaves in the winter, is to experience wonder. Bonsai allows a pause in the relentless pace of daily life, and contact with nature's great calm. This is its essence.

When bonsai were first exhibited in the Western world around the turn of the century, they were greeted with a feeling of astonishment and a sense of awe. After the exhibitions were over, the bonsai were not returned to Japan but were sold in the country where the plants had been shown. When many of these trees died because the new owners did not have the knowledge to properly care for them, the original fascination soon gave way to the question, "How do you keep them alive?"

The science of horticulture provides the basic guidance for all bonsai artists to produce and maintain their bonsai. The most important horticultural information required is the knowledge needed to keep the bonsai alive. In reality, this is no mystery. Bonsai are like every other living organism. Provide them with the correct environmental conditions and they will thrive. In fact, bonsai, when properly cared for, will live far longer than their counterparts growing in nature. All bonsai artists, however, use the science of horticulture far more extensively than to just keep their bonsai alive. By understanding the growth habits of the plant, the artist can manipulate and harness those characteristics to help create a particular bonsai shape.

Both artistic vision and horticultural techniques are required to produce the illusion of a large old tree growing in nature, from a bonsai only inches high. Since bonsai artists, by necessity, work through the seasons and years to develop their bonsai, it can take a very long time to accumulate the

All the majesty and character of an ancient tree is captured in this gnarled old pomegranate, although it is no more than 18 inches tall.

enthusiast. By sharing his years of experience, his horticultural knowledge, his artistic insight, and his enthusiasm, he will enable the beginner to start the process of learning about bonsai with a wealth of sound information. In addition, he also presents a comprehensive and concise section that provides advice on specific plants that are often used for commercial bonsai. This is invaluable when you are faced with a plant species with which you are not familiar, or when you are looking for help in keeping your bonsai alive and healthy.

Bonsai, although an ancient art, is very appropriate to modern times. Man is attempting to forge a new relationship with nature, a oneness combining his concept of beauty with the mysteries of the natural world. Participation in this wonderful and fascinating hobby provides all of us with an opportunity to achieve happiness that money cannot buy nor power command. Welcome to the wonderful world of bonsai.

necessary experience and knowledge. Having a good teacher, whether in person or through the medium of the printed word, is absolutely essential to the process of learning about bonsai.

That is where this book by Mr. Colin Lewis will be of great benefit to the novice bonsai

Jack Douthitt

Jack Douthitt

INTRODUCTION

LEFT
The interplay between trees, water and man-made hills has for centuries played a significant role in Chinese and Japanese landscape design, as shown in this illustration of the Imperial Gardens in Peking. These simple elements are the basic components of all bonsai design, regardless of its origin or style.

ABOVE RIGHT
A private collection of tropical bonsai, including several varieties of fig. Every available space is used as the collection increases steadily year after year.

SINCE ITS BEGINNINGS in China, during the Han Dynasty over two thousand years ago, the art of growing miniaturized trees in containers has undergone a highly checkered history. For a time, bonsai, or *penjing* as the Chinese call it, was regarded as too spiritually enriching for the masses, and only those of noble birth were permitted to own one. Legend has it that at one point an ancient Chinese Emperor commissioned the construction in his courtyard of vast miniature landscapes, complete with mountains, lakes and, of course, miniature trees. These landscapes were designed to represent all the parts of his empire, so in this way he could stand on his balcony and survey his entire domain. Anyone else who had the nerve to own even a modest miniature landscape in a dish was deemed to represent a

threat to his authority and was immediately branded a traitor and put to death.

In the fourteenth century the Chinese invaded Japan and took with them many aspects of Chinese culture, including religion, calligraphy and *penjing*. Even today the Japanese characters for bonsai remain the same as the Chinese. In typical fashion, the Japanese developed and refined this fascinating art, but it was not a straightforward process at all. For many years bonsai remained the privilege of the noblemen, so when they began to lose interest, it almost died out altogether, and was only practiced by a few people. Once again bonsai rose in popularity, but this time enthusiasts were more concerned with colored flowers and variegated leaves than they were with the shape or realism of the tree. This approach was clearly subject to changes in fashion, so once again the popularity of bonsai declined.

The development of bonsai as we now know it really began during the last century. The Japanese love of nature, their increasing artistic awareness and the minimalist teachings of Zen Buddhism combined to influence the further evolution of bonsai to the sophisticated art form that it is in Japan today.

But there was one more trauma to overcome. In the 1920s, a massive earthquake devastated the main bonsai growing area in the north. Many major collections were

Bon (tree)

Sai (pot)

totally destroyed and many of the most accomplished artists lost their lives. Undeterred, a handful of the remaining artists joined together to form another community, this time in Omiya, just outside Tokyo. This bonsai village still exists, although it has now become a suburb of Tokyo. One of the original artists still lives there, and Omiya has become a mecca and attracts serious bonsai enthusiasts from the four corners of the world.

The journey West

Although Westerners had encountered bonsai on their travels in the Far East, and a few had written about them in scholarly journals, it was not until the end of World War II that the hobby began to catch on in the West. GIs returning from Japan brought with them small examples of these fascinating little trees. Of course, many of them only survived for a short time, but there were enough people curious enough to try to discover how to care for them properly. The large Japanese-American population in the United States was the major source of information and encouragement, and for many years their knowledge and skills were in demand throughout the Western world.

Today, "bonsai" has become a household word. Small cuttings planted in shallow pots are sold as bonsai in department stores, garden nurseries, open air markets and even in gas stations. These are a far cry from the true bonsai that are produced by artists in many western countries as well as Japan. But they are a start. They at least introduce newcomers to the idea of growing a miniaturized tree in a pot. It is then up to the individual to read books, join clubs and meet and talk with other bonsai enthusiasts in order to learn and improve his or her skills.

This book is the first step on that road. It gives you all the

LEFT
Specimen bonsai
neatly displayed in
one of the many fine
nurseries in Omiya
Bonsai Village,
Japan, which has
become the Mecca
for bonsai enthusiasts
from all corners of
the world.

RIGHT
The grotesque,
almost animal-like
trunk and writhing,
exposed roots are
typical of classical
Chinese bonsai.

information you will need to ensure
that your first few bonsai trees will
flourish, regardless of how much
they cost. The knowledge gained
here will enable you to develop your
trees with confidence over the years.
As your enthusiasm grows, you may
become more ambitious and begin
to create your own bonsai from
native plants, or you may simply be
content to maintain your first trees
in perfect condition. Either way, you
will find the art of bonsai a most
absorbing and satisfying pastime.

BELOW RIGHT
With evenly formed
roots and precisely
controlled branch
placement, this
classical Japanese
trident maple is
resplendent in full
autumn color.

CHAPTER ONE

BUYING BONSAI

Buying a bonsai is a commitment – very much like buying a pet – as it will need daily attention. It needs food and water, it will require trimming every few weeks in the spring and the summer, it should be repotted periodically and it must be kept free of all pests and diseases.

The roots of this trident maple have been tightly clasping the rock for so long that they are now beginning to mesh together, and will eventually totally engulf the rock. This is the ever-changing art of bonsai.

BEFORE YOU BUY

A BONSAI PLANT must be given the appropriate environmental conditions if it is to survive for long. I am frequently asked at public bonsai exhibitions: "Why did my bonsai die?" As often as not, the answer is that the poor little tree was placed in an entirely inappropriate situation. Pines, which thrive on having their roots frozen solid for a time over winter, will die within a week or two if kept too near a radiator in a living room. The Fukien tea (*Carmona microphylla*) wouldn't even survive a single light frost. So many have died when left outside and caught by an unexpected drop in temperature.

Where to buy?
Once you have decided what growing conditions you can offer, you then have to decide upon a suitable dealer. It is always best to buy from dealers specializing in bonsai for a number of reasons:
- They know their products.
- They can offer expert advice.
- They want you to come back, so will not sell you a sick tree.
- They will give you accurate care information.
- They normally offer a selection of tools, books and magazines to help you create and care for your bonsai.

Specialist nurseries are very careful to stock only those species

they know will thrive either in the local climate if kept outdoors, or under normal conditions in the average home in your part of the country. Finally, you can be confident that if you do encounter a problem with your tree, you will be able to return to the nursery for help – many even offer "hospital" and vacation care services.

Although the bonsai offered for sale in garden nurseries and florists in shopping malls and elsewhere are generally healthy and well cared for, they do tend to be overpriced. Such places rely on sales volume, so they prefer to sell a hundred small bonsai rather than ten larger ones. And

WHERE TO PUT YOUR BONSAI

Before you buy your bonsai, consider the conditions it will have to tolerate:

- Do you want to keep it outdoors?
- If so, how cold are your winters? They may be too cold for some species but not cold enough for others.
- Do you want to keep it indoors? If so, where?
- Is your house/apartment heated?
- Do you have a well-lit room or are all your windows facing away from the sun?
- Can you provide a frost-free environment in winter?

Commercial tropical bonsai are kept protected and in peak condition in an environmentally controlled greenhouse at Tokonoma Bonsai Nursery in the UK.

This poor, ugly little privet (*Ligustrum*) could spend months trapped in its dark, suffocating box, and is already showing signs of stress. Never buy "bonsai" pre-packaged like this.

since bonsai have a reputation for being expensive, a simple rooted cutting in a shallow pot is sold at twenty times its real value. Having said this, you may be lucky and pick up a bargain.

Department stores, farmers' markets and any of the other unlikely places that bonsai are sold should be avoided. Here again, you may be lucky enough to buy a plant that will live, but the vast majority are dying before they are bought. The employees will know little about plants and nothing about bonsai. You will probably be given all kinds of incorrect information in the salesperson's desperation to earn a commission. As a result of your disappointment, you will turn your back on bonsai for ever and will miss out on a wealth of pleasure and satisfaction. Mail order is a risky way to buy bonsai. Not only will you be buying bonsai unseen, but it may suffer in the post. If you buy mail-order, be sure to buy only from a specialist bonsai dealer.

WHICH SPECIES?

Having decided on the environmental conditions you can offer your bonsai, you may then select a suitable species. There are three categories:

Tropical plants
These require constant high temperatures and generally prefer high humidity. They also prefer high light levels, unless they are forest floor dwellers in the wild. They cannot tolerate cold and many will die if exposed to temperatures below 50°F for any length of time. They are referred to as "tender" species.

A tropical cycas

Subtropical plants
These plants originate from Californian- or Mediterranean-type climates. They also like high temperatures, but prefer cooler, drier conditions in the dormant season. Some subtropicals can tolerate a degree or so below freezing for very short periods, and are known as "half-hardy" plants. Others will suffer after overnight exposure to temperatures below 45°F, and will die if exposed to frost. Like the tropicals, these are tender species. All subtropicals react badly to dry, overheated rooms and need spraying with fresh water two or three times a day.

A subtropical olive

Temperate plants
These include all bonsai exported from Japan, which like most of North America and Europe, has a temperate climate. The summers are warm and wet and the winters have prolonged periods below freezing. Trees adapted to this climate often deteriorate if they do not receive sufficient winter cold. They die of exhaustion if deprived of their essential winter rest period by being kept indoors. Even in summer, they prefer to be outside. Indoors the light level is always considerably lower, causing weak, "leggy" growth and large, thin, pale leaves. These plants are referred to as "hardy" species.

A hardy stewartia

WHAT TO LOOK FOR

HERE YOU CAN let your taste dictate. There are many different styles of bonsai ranging from the neat, formalized Japanese trees to the bizarre, sometimes animal-like Chinese *penjing*. Provided the species suits the place you have chosen for it, you are free to select a shape that captures your imagination.

But before taking the final decision, there are a few points to check. Once you get your bonsai home, and have studied it for a while, you may begin to notice irritating little faults that were not apparent in the nursery. Many of these can be corrected in time, but it is obviously better to avoid them in the first place.

Root formation

The exposed surface roots should appear natural as they spread out from the trunk and thrust into the soil. Some styles have a lot of exposed roots which lift the trunk above the level of the ground. These sometimes become contorted and tangled, which is fine so long as they are natural looking and there are no heavy pruning scars. In the long term, it is best to go for the natural rather than the grotesque.

Trunk line

An even taper from the base to the crown is ideal. There should be no

A GOOD BUY
This red maple is only slightly more expensive than the one opposite, but it is much better value for several reasons.

The foliage is healthy and dense, and even the lower shoots are growing vigorously – this is a sure sign of good health.

The odd weed or two in the pot means that the soil is moist but not waterlogged.

The trunk is sturdy and flares nicely into reasonably well positioned, spreading roots. If they were just planted a little deeper . . . .

LEFT
Branches can easily be altered; roots are much more difficult to change. If you spot a heavy trunk with uniform yet natural rootage like this, buy it quickly before anyone else does!

A BAD BUY
This unfortunate red maple has no real branch structure, just young shoots growing from knotty stumps.

If left on for too long, wire will cut into the bark as the branch thickens, leaving scars that will never completely disappear. In extreme cases, the branch may die.

The skinny trunk is actually thicker in the middle than it is at the base.

There are no visible surface roots, which are essential in good bonsai. The soil has been mounded up around the trunk in an effort to conceal thin or ugly roots.

Careless pruning leaves scars that never heal well. Even if carved out now, there would still be an ugly swelling around the wound for many years.

PLANTS TO AVOID

If you buy from a reputable specialist nursery, or even from a garden nursery, the plant should be in good health and pest-free. Nevertheless, it is wise to check it out before spending your money.

- Dry or yellowing foliage, dead shoots, powdery deposits on the leaves and twisted or stunted new shoots are all signs of fungal infections or infestations of minute insects. Most are easily cured, but that is the grower's job, not yours, so don't buy.

- Avoid buying deciduous, hardy trees in winter because it is not so easy to judge their health – or even if they are still alive. Scratching away a little bark to see if the tissue beneath is green – as it should be – is one way to tell, but don't let the store owner see you do it!

- Moss on the surface of the soil is a sign that the bonsai is established in the pot. The odd weed or two won't hurt, but too many weeds are a sign of neglect. The soil should not appear to be compacted and hard. It should be moist, not bone dry or waterlogged. *Gently* try to rock the tree in the pot – if it feels loose, then the roots are not well established, so put it back on the shelf.

visible heavy pruning scars unless they can be disguised and made more natural by hollowing them out. Many bonsai are produced by chopping the top off a larger tree and growing branches on the stump. This can leave an ugly square top to the trunk which may be hidden beneath the foliage. If this cut is made at an angle, it will eventually blend in with the trunk line, but if it is made straight across the trunk, it will never improve.

Branch structure

Keep in mind that the general shape of the tree will change within a week or two as the growing shoots lengthen. Although the shape of the crown is important, it is not as important as the placement and shape of the branches that support it. If you have a good branch structure, you can easily trim the foliage to a good shape. Branches are shaped by coiling wire around them to hold them in position until they "set." You can do this, too, to improve the branch structure. However, if the wire is left on for too long, it will cut into the bark, causing scars that will never fully heal. Unfortunately, many commercial growers allow this to happen, and some unscrupulous dealers pass it off as an aging technique or part of the intended style. Don't believe them – wire scars are *always* a flaw in a bonsai and can ruin an otherwise perfect little tree.

It is very unlikely that you will find the perfect bonsai. There will almost certainly be too many branches, especially at the top. Spend some time thinking about how you could, by pruning and wire-shaping, create a more realistic and pleasing branch structure than what you see in front of you at the store.

EVALUATING BRANCH STRUCTURE

Here are a few tips on evaluating the branch structure of a bonsai:
- The lower branches should be the heaviest ones on the tree.
- Branches should be evenly distributed around the trunk.
- They should emerge from the trunk in a natural way.
- There should be no wire cutting into the bark or scars caused by wire that was left on too long.

An unusual formal upright elm with branches positioned along textbook lines. The tree is photographed from the back, so that you can see the position of the lowest back branch.

Note how the lower branches are horizontal, but the higher branches sweep gently upwards.

The trunk is bolt upright, with an even taper extending from base to apex.

Price

Bonsai are expensive in comparison with other plants, but that does not mean they are overpriced. They can take a relatively long time to produce and have to be shipped halfway around the world to reach you. Of course, some are better value than others, and if you follow the tips given above, you are likely to get a good deal. The best advice here is to decide how much you want to spend before you go, and stick to it. It is all too easy to get carried away with the magic of these little trees, and take a snap decision you may regret later.

When all is said and done, the most important thing is that you are happy with your choice. Take your tree home, treasure it and care for it every day, and it will reward you with years of pleasure and satisfaction.

20 DOS AND DON'TS OF BUYING BONSAI

DO shop around – visit more than one outlet.

DO buy only from specialist nurseries.

DO decide what you want to spend before you go.

DO choose a species that suits the conditions you can offer and check the accuracy of the labels.

DO study each tree carefully, checking for ugly scars or wire marks.

DO check the foliage for fungal or insect attack, especially underneath and toward the center of the tree.

DO gently rock the tree to ensure it is firm in its pot.

DO ask the dealer to ease the tree out of its pot to check that the roots are healthy. If they are dull and brown, or if you can't see any, don't buy.

DO check the pot has adequate drainage holes.

DO ask about the trees' origins, recent history, last repotting, etc. And ask for a care information leaflet – all good nurseries should have them.

DON'T buy a bonsai from a source that doesn't have an established reputation.

DON'T buy from an outlet where the salespeople do not seem knowledgeable about bonsai.

DON'T buy pre-packaged bonsai or bonsai in display boxes.

DON'T believe the stated age. Most dealers tend to exaggerate.

DON'T buy any tree with saturated or poorly drained soil.

DON'T buy a tree with dry or discolored foliage, or any other sign of ill health.

DON'T buy any tree that is not firm in its pot.

DON'T buy any tree with wire cutting into the bark.

DON'T buy a species you are not confident about, *and*

DON'T buy a bonsai if it doesn't look like a real little tree. You are paying for the skill and expertise of the grower, and you are entitled to expect him or her to do a proper job.

Healthy foliage, a neat outline, and an overall realistic impression make this maple group highly desirable.

This unfortunate privet, with its odd roots, untapered trunk, lack of real branches, and sickly foliage is ideally suited to the tacky pot and ridiculous miniature temple on the rock.

CHAPTER TWO

CARING FOR YOUR BONSAI

In the most basic terms, bonsai are only potted plants and, provided you follow the simple advice in this chapter, and you approach them with the same confidence that you have when caring for your other potted plants, you won't go too far wrong. The only significant differences are that they are regularly shaped and they are generally planted in shallow containers.

Looking after a bonsai means striking the right balance of water, temperature, air, and light for each species. This fig is producing masses of aerial roots, just like it would in the wild – a sure sign of health.

WHERE TO KEEP YOUR BONSAI

WE HAVE DISCUSSED the difference between so-called "indoor" and "outdoor" bonsai in Chapter One. Regardless of whether your bonsai is hardy, half-hardy or tender, the main consideration is to keep it as near as possible in the type of environment that particular species enjoys in the wild. Detailed advice on individual species is given in the Species Profiles (pages 56–157), so here we will deal with the importance of various environmental factors to your trees.

Light and shade

All plants require light so that their leaves can produce essential sugars through photosynthesis. Without sufficient light, the new growth will become "leggy" in an attempt to grow taller to reach the light through what the plant assumes to be a canopy of older trees. Eventually the new shoots, which will be paler green than normal, will outgrow their own strength and will collapse and die. Without the new leaves to manufacture sugars, the plant will become undernourished and it, too, will eventually die.

On the other hand, some plants are accustomed to living on the margins of woods, where they are in dappled shade. Others have adapted to life in deeper shade, although none of the species commonly sold

as bonsai fall into this category.

No plants grown in pots of any kind enjoy too much sun – the pot and roots overheat, which reduces their efficiency, and the foliage becomes deprived of moisture in consequence. The leaves wilt and become scorched and curl at the edges, reducing their efficiency and damaging the tree's health.

The worst possible position for any bonsai, indoors or outdoors, is where it is shaded for the early part of the day and is suddenly exposed to full sun in the afternoon. This sudden shock to the leaves can cause severe scorching and even total defoliation. For this reason, when putting tender trees, which are kept indoors in the winter, outside in the summer, they must be gradually acclimatized by increasing

DISPLAYING BONSAI

Bonsai mostly live in situations that favor their general well-being. But each bonsai is a work of art, and from time to time you will want to display it as such. In Japan, bonsai are displayed in a special wide alcove called a *tokanoma*, which can take up almost the entire wall of a room.

• The bonsai always stand on a low table or polished wooden base of some kind. On the wall behind the tree, slightly to one side, is a single scroll containing some calligraphy or a simple brush drawing. The third, stabilizing element in the composition is an accent plant – a grass, wild flower or fern, or a viewing stone or *suiseki*, whose shape represents a distant mountain. You don't have to go to this extent, but many bonsai enthusiasts have a quiet corner of the house where they can display their tree-of-the-moment in isolation for a few days.

• If you want to display outdoor bonsai inside, limit the time to two or

three days in the summer, and only a few hours during the winter. A longer time away from their usual environment will interfere with the tree's growth pattern.

A Japanese-style *tokanoma*, or alcove. The scroll represents the sky, and the rock represents the earth. The bonsai is nature, linking the two.

LEFT
Most homes have a quiet corner with a plain background that can be used for temporary display of the bonsai-of-the-moment.

RIGHT
A Western bonsai garden belonging to British bonsai teacher, Dan Barton. Most of these hardy bonsai will spend all year on their stands – only the maples will be protected for a couple of months.

their exposure to full sun a little each day.

When plants are pampered indoors all winter, their leaves become soft and delicate, and are easily damaged by sudden exposure to the real world outside. Sun is not the only element you must watch. Wind can also dry foliage rapidly and, unless your bonsai has had time to acclimatize, its leaves will surely suffer in a spring breeze. Even trees which have been allowed to come into leaf in a polyethylene shelter will scorch if introduced to the open air too suddenly.

Temperature

As with light, a sudden change in temperature is dangerous for any plant. If plants are kept on a bright windowsill, it may be as hot as a desert during the day, but at night the temperature between the glass and the curtain may drop to within a degree or so of freezing. This is fine for some cacti, but not for bonsai. Always try to maintain even temperatures and make sure that any changes in temperature are gradual.

Placing indoor trees on a low

Delicate Japanese maple leaves are easily scorched by sun or drying winds even when temperatures are not particularly high.

The tall trees behind this display help shelter the bonsai from sun and wind. The more delicate species are placed on the lower level for additional protection.

Bad position for indoor bonsai
Sunlight passing through a window becomes intensified and much hotter (which is why greenhouses work!). This position may suit cacti but not bonsai in their fragile micro-environment.

Pressed against the window pane, like this, a bonsai would soon become parched and die.

At night, when the curtains are closed, the temperature between the curtains and the window can fall dramatically.

The upward draft of hot air while the radiator is on will dry the soil – and leaves – in a matter of just a few hours.

table a few feet from the window ensures that both light and temperature are fairly even throughout the day. Keep them far away from sources of heat like radiators, water heaters, etc., and never put them on the television set!

Humidity

The fact that bonsai are grown in shallow containers means that their roots have to work extra hard to supply the rest of the plant with adequate moisture. On warm days, especially if there is a stiff breeze, the leaves may lose moisture through evaporation faster than the roots can supply it.

Trees kept outside are generally tougher and in hot dry weather their leaves harden and the pores (stomata) close. This helps reduce moisture loss, but also slows down the trees' metabolism. Standing your display tables on wet gravel can help to create a more humid local environment and assist in reducing moisture loss. Spraying the foliage of the bonsai with rainwater two or three times during the day is always a good idea.

Trees kept indoors can be placed on stones in a tray of wet gravel or decorative pebbles. This, too, will create a humid micro-environment. Spraying the foliage as often as possible will keep the leaves in good condition. However, if you live in an area where water from the faucet is hard (water with a high lime content), constant spraying will leave deposits of white calcium on the leaf edges and on flaky bark. This doesn't harm the tree, but it is unsightly and difficult to remove.

Hard water (water containing lime) often leaves a crusty deposit of calcium on the exposed roots and lower trunk. Vigorous brushing with a hard toothbrush eventually removes it.

Filtered water or rainwater are ideal for spraying.

Air

Plants need air to breathe, just as we do. The local air quality will affect the health of trees as well as animals and humans. An indoor tree that lives in a smoky, too well heated and

Good position for indoor bonsai
A bright, airy room is ideal for all plants, not only bonsai. Further away from the window, the intensity of the sun is decreased to an acceptable level and the temperature is more constant.

The venetian blind can be adjusted to provide the right amount of dappled shade when necessary. Turning the tree from time to time ensures that it receives even light all around.

The TV is the focal point in many rooms, but is the worst possible place for a bonsai. It is too warm, and you should never water a tree sitting on top of an electrical appliance. It could prove fatal to you and the tree.

poorly ventilated room wouldn't last more than a few weeks. Even air conditioning doesn't provide perfect air, but it certainly helps.

Outdoor trees living close to heavy traffic or in areas of heavy industrial pollution also suffer, just like their full-sized cousins. Using collected rainwater in such areas can even compound the problem as that, too, will probably be polluted.

Naturally, you are not going to move to a new house for the sake of your bonsai, but an awareness of local air quality may influence your choice of species.

All trees appreciate fresh air, so rooms containing bonsai should have good ventilation. Leave doors open as much as possible to ensure good air circulation *but not drafts*! A cool draft will both chill and dry a tree at the same time, and the ill effects will become noticeable after a few hours in some cases. Poor air circulation around the foliage can encourage fungal diseases such as mildew, or attacks by some pests like red spider mites.

Plants kept at ground level are subjected to the coldest air and the poorest air circulation. Indoors, keep your bonsai on a table or sideboard – a low coffee table might be too low for the tree's comfort. Outdoors, trees should be kept on slatted benches, raised to at least table height. This also protects them from slugs, snails, and the neighbour's cat, as well as raising them to a more practical level for appreciation and maintenance.

Whether trees are kept indoors or outside, they should be sheltered from strong breezes at all times.

Protecting hardy trees in winter
All hardy trees can withstand having their roots frozen solid for short periods. Conifers are active throughout the winter, but they generally have waxy coatings on the leaves which protect them against frost and reduce moisture loss. Deciduous trees, although dormant in winter, still need water to maintain life. All trees can lose

Trees with fleshy roots can have their roots protected by wrapping the pot in several layers of burlap, which allows air and water to pass through but provides adequate insulation.

moisture slowly through the bark, so if the roots are unable to take up water because they are frozen for long periods, the tree may suffer from the effects of drought.

The main enemy of hardy trees in winter is not the temperature but the drying wind, so all hardy bonsai must be sheltered from wind at this time. Evergreens can be placed in the shelter of a wall or fence, or on the ground between the display benches. Deciduous trees, especially those with thick, fleshy roots such as trident maples and Chinese elms, will need some additional protection.

A polyethylene greenhouse or even a makeshift polyethylene tent would be ideal, provided that it is not allowed to heat up too much on sunny days, and that the air is changed by opening the door for a while each day. Since deciduous trees don't require light in the dormant season, they can even be stored in a dark garden shed or garage until the moment when the buds show signs of swelling.

LEFT
A makeshift shelter of clear plastic draped over the display benches may not look pretty, but it provides perfect protection from winter wind and excessive rain.

THE GROWING RISK OF THEFT

It is sad to say that each year that passes brings an increase in the number of thefts of bonsai, particularly from back yards. Equally sadly, there is very little you can do to prevent theft, apart from the usual garden or domestic security measures.

Insurance companies are not prepared to provide cover for bonsai, and the recovery rate for stolen trees is very low. Most of them die before the thief can dispose of them.

The best advice is.
• Never boast about your bonsai collection in front of people you don't know well.
• Never exaggerate the value of your bonsai.

I have a friend who had many of his best trees stolen from his yard one night. In order to motivate the police to recover them, he exaggerated their value tenfold. The total was so great that it made the front page of the local newspaper. Sure, he motivated the police, and his trees were recovered. However, he also motivated every petty crook in the area, and caused a spate of similar thefts. Needless to say, none of the other stolen trees were returned to their owners.

WATERING

1 If your bonsai does accidentally dry out completely, follow this procedure and you stand a good chance of saving it. If the casualty is a broad-leaved tree, remove all remaining leaves to reduce further moisture loss.

BONSAI NEED water to survive. The problem is that many novices are so concerned about not giving their tree enough water that they overdo it. It is ironic, but more bonsai are killed through drowning than by drought.

When to water

Species with shiny, waxy leaves are adapted to conserve water, so they will need watering less often. Those with soft-surfaced, thin leaves tend to lose moisture through evaporation more rapidly and will need more frequent watering.

Never wait until the soil is bone dry before watering. For one thing, if the roots dry out completely for a short time, the fine feeding roots will die and debilitate the plant. Some species, especially those which prefer damp conditions in the wild, will even die if allowed to dry out for only a day or so. Another reason is that soil becomes very difficult to wet once it has become bone dry. It may seem as if the water has penetrated the soil, but the central core may remain dry as the water runs down between the soil and the inside of the pot.

By the same token, if the soil is still very wet, do not water. Waterlogged conditions literally drown the roots – they are unable to breathe and begin to rot, and the tree is unable to take up water even though the soil is wet.

Ideally, the soil should become just moist between thorough waterings. As each plant is different, and is growing in unique conditions, it is impossible to give specific timing. Your experience will soon tell you when the time is right.

How to water

Use a watering can with a fine rose indoors or a hose with a fine spray attachment for outdoor collections. Water the soil first, until the water covers the surface and reaches the rim of the pot. Allow this water to soak through and then repeat the process. You should now see water draining through the holes in the base of the pot. If not, repeat the process once more. Finally, spray the foliage to refresh the leaves.

If the soil seems to become dry quicker than it should, try standing the pot in a bowl of water for half an hour. This should solve the problem. If it doesn't, it is more than likely that the tree's roots have become pot-bound. Under these circumstances, the root mass is so dense that there is little space for water or air, and the tree should be repotted and root pruned at the earliest appropriate time. Planting the tree in a larger, temporary container, such as a seed tray, is a sensible interim measure.

Overhead spraying and watering

Immersion watering technique

SAVING A DRIED-OUT TREE

2 Immerse the pot in a bowl of clean water deep enough to cover the soil completely. Leave immersed for about half an hour.

3 Remove the pot from the water and stand it with one end raised to help the excess water drain away.

4 Place the tree and pot in a clear polyethylene bag and seal it. Ensure that the bag is not in contact with any part of the tree, or it will encourage decay. Don't feed until new growth appears. This may take from a few days to several months.

Vacation care

Many nurseries offer a reasonably priced vacation care service where you can be confident your trees will be well looked after. Fellow bonsai enthusiasts are also a safe bet.

Friends and neighbors often feel privileged when asked to water bonsai, but beware. If you do ask an inexperienced neighbor to water while you are away, give them plenty of notice and practice. Teach them how to water properly and make them aware of how important correct watering is. Remember, although a bonsai can die of drought within twenty-four hours, a week or two of overwatering will also kill it.

An alternative solution is to bury the pots in a moist, shady corner so that the surface of the soil in the pot is covered by about ½ inch of earth. This should keep the pots moist for a week or two. Take precautions against slugs and cats.

CAPILLARY WATERING

If there is no one to care for your bonsai in your absence, a system of capillary watering can prevent serious drought for a week or two. Capillary matting is very much like felt, and is used mainly in greenhouses to water plant pots and seed beds. It is readily available in most garden nurseries and stores.

- Cut a piece of matting to fit snugly in the base of the pot.
- Cut some strips, about 1 inch wide and insert one through each drainage hole, so that about 2 inches lies between the inside of the pot and the matting.
- Place the pot on a flat surface and trail the other ends of the matting strips into a reservoir of water. The strips of matting will act as wicks and slowly draw water into the pot.

This setup is far from ideal, but it should prevent the pot from drying out completely for as long as the reservoir lasts. As an extra precaution, if the trees are kept indoors, close all windows and doors and place some

Strips of capillary matting draw water into the base of the pot which is lined with more matting.

bowls of water nearby to maintain humidity. Outside, trees should be put in full shade, or preferably a shaded tent of polyethylene. Covering the surfaces of the pots with loose sphagnum moss or a thick layer of bark clippings will reduce evaporation.

FEEDING YOUR BONSAI

IF YOU ASK in a dozen different garden stores: "What is a good fertilizer for bonsai?", you would probably get a dozen different answers. The range of commercial plant feeds is bewildering – some for house plants, some for roses, some for lawns and so on. However, they all contain just three basic elements in various proportions, plus a few trace elements.

How to feed

Provided you follow the instructions on the package, you will keep your tree healthy – perhaps a little too healthy. Trees in general are not hungry plants in the way roses or tomatoes are. Overfeeding a bonsai will cause the leaves to become too large and the new shoots too vigorous.

Never use more than the recommended amount of fertilizer. Instead of giving your tree a boost, it will "burn" the roots and do more harm than good.

Special bonsai fertilizers should always be used at the recommended dose, but house plant and garden fertilizers are best used at half strength, but twice as often. This is because the recommended dose is for deeper pots which are not regularly flushed out with fresh water.

Liquid fertilizers can either be watered into the soil or sprayed on

ESSENTIAL PLANT FOODS

Somewhere on the packages of all fertilisers you will find the N.P.K. analysis. This indicates the proportions of the three essential nutrients:

- "N" stands for nitrogen, which is mainly responsible for leaf and stem growth, and giving good healthy color. Lawn feeds contain a high proportion of nitrogen.

- "P" stands for phosphorus, which builds sturdy roots and trunks. It also greatly enhances a plant's resistance to disease.

- "K" stands for potassium (from the Latin word *kalium*), which is the main flower-inducing nutrient. It also helps strengthen roots and young shoots ready for winter.

Fertilizers for fruiting and flowering plants have high proportions of potassium and phosphorus.

Trace elements are only required in minute quantities, but they are nevertheless essential for healthy plants. Read the labels carefully and make sure that the fertilizer you are buying contains at least some of the six major trace elements.

For all but flowering bonsai, a balanced feed is ideal, with an N.P.K. analysis of roughly equal proportions of each. Whether the actual numbers are low (e.g. 3:4:4) or high (e.g. 24:20:20) doesn't matter – the dilution instructions on the package allow for this. Generally speaking, most house plant fertilizers are fine for small collections of bonsai.

Nitrogen encourages lush foliage and young shoots

Phosphorus strengthens roots and trunks

Potassium helps produce flowers and fruit

THE FEEDING CYCLE

Spring
● Begin feeding after the first few new leaves have appeared at the start of the growing season. By this time, your tree will have used some of its stored energy and is ready for more.

Summer
● By midsummer, trees which flower in the spring are beginning to set new flower buds for next year. This is the time to reduce the N and increase the P and K Greenhouse tomato feed is perfect for this purpose if diluted and applied as recommended above.

Fall
● Toward the end of the growing season, apply a nitrogen-free fertilizer if possible. This will prevent any new growth which may die back during the colder months, and harden existing roots and shoots.

Winter
● Since evergreens are slightly active all year round, an application of very diluted, low nitrogen feed once a month in winter will get the tree off to a good start in the spring.

the leaves. Plants can actually absorb more nutrients through their leaves than through their roots. Foliar feeding is quick and convenient, but it does tend to leave white powdery deposits on the leaves. The major advantage of liquid feeds is that you can control when and how much is given.

Pelleted fertilizers are my choice, simply because they only need to be applied once or twice a year. Also, you wash nutrients into the soil each time you water, not out of it as with a liquid feed. If you use pellets, make sure that they are intended for container-grown plants. Garden fertilizer pellets may have a low N.P.K., but they are intended to nourish large areas of deep ground and are far too concentrated for container-grown bonsai.

Pellets can either be mixed with the soil at repotting or applied to the surface. I prefer the latter because I can ensure that they are evenly distributed. Pressing the pellets into the soil stops them being washed off with overzealous watering.

When to feed
Plants are opportunists – they take up whatever nutrients are offered, whether they need them or not. They store a certain amount in the trunk and roots; the rest is channeled into producing more tissue of one form or another. Too much of the wrong ingredient, or feeding at the wrong time, may encourage the tree into an

unseasonal growth pattern, which can be harmful. Refer to the Species Profiles for detailed feeding programs for individual species.
● Only feed the tree when it is in active growth.
● Don't feed for three weeks after repotting.
● Stop feeding deciduous trees *before* the leaves turn to a fall color.

Slow-release fertilizer pellets can be gently pressed into the surface of the soil to stop them being washed away during watering.

CHAPTER THREE

SHAPING YOUR BONSAI

*Once it starts growing, the shape of your bonsai rapidly changes.
A miniature tree can become a ragged bush in just a few weeks.
You soon discover that owning a bonsai is an active hobby! At first
you will probably want to maintain the tree's original shape.
After a while, when you know every branch and twig
intimately, you may decide to modify the shape
somehow – a longer branch here, or a bit more
space there. There may be a branch that is
too straight or too many in one area.*

Most commercial bonsai, like this pistachio,
resemble a little tree. But within a month
or so they will have become overgrown
and will need to be trimmed or even
reshaped. Each time you do so you
will make improvements.

SHAPING YOUR NEW BONSAI

WHEN YOU ACQUIRE a new bonsai, it should have a pleasing tree-like shape. Don't be too concerned if the leaves begin to fall, or if some tender young shoots die back. A sudden change in environment causes stress which will have a visible effect on most trees. Leaf shedding and shoot dieback are safety mechanisms designed to reduce moisture loss through the leaves and to conserve energy in times of stress.

As time passes the trunk will gradually thicken and the tree might slowly increase in size. The pot may no longer be big enough for the tree – horticulturally or visually – so you will need to select a better one. As each year passes, the bonsai reflects

ACCLIMATIZING BONSAI

Don't take panic measures with a new bonsai such as:

- Overwatering
- Giving extra fertilizer
- Putting the tree on a sunny windowsill
- Giving it extra heat.

Leave the tree in a position where it will receive good light but no direct sun, and positively no draft or wind. It will soon recover, and you can then introduce it to its permanent position – for a couple of hours at first, increasing the time each day for a week or so, until it is fully acclimatized.

more of your personality and what was once someone else's little creation becomes your work of art.

What shape?

The general shape will have been decided by the original grower, based on the shape of the trunk.

Chinese and Korean bonsai – tropical and subtropical species – commonly have tangled, exposed roots, often with dramatically shaped trunks. In China, bonsai with trunks that look like animals or birds are popular. There is often some equally dramatic rock in the pot and small figures or temples. These trinkets are aimed at the Western market, but they are seldom in proportion to the tree and detract from the composition.

Specimen Chinese and Korean bonsai, those for collectors or museums, do not have such ornaments. They are large, imposing and heavy-trunked, but still reflect the dragon-like quality of the commercial trees. The lines and foliage masses are flowing and free.

Specimen Japanese bonsai are heavily stylized and refined. The Japanese have classified bonsai into over a dozen clearly defined styles, ranging from *Chokkan* (formal upright) through *Bunjingi*

("literati," or slender trunk) to *Yose-ue* (forest). Every branch, twig and shoot is immaculately controlled.

Commercial Japanese bonsai are not so refined, unless you are prepared to spend a lot of money. However, they are all grown with one of the classical styles in mind, and should provide you with the basic framework which you can develop to create the finer details.

In bonsai, natural shapes have been classified into a number of distinct styles, based in the main on the shape of the trunk. These styles form the ideal shapes which all bonsai should aim to achieve.

Twisted trunk, or *bankan* style, more popular in China than Japan

Slanting, reminiscent of the lower mountain slopes

Exposed root, from the river banks and scree slopes

Root over rock, another style of river bank or rocky slope origin

Root on rock, the rock becomes the pot and a dramatic scene is created

Driftwood, based on mountain junipers, this style is almost abstract art

Formal upright, the trunk is ramrod straight and evenly tapered

Semi-cascade, where the lowest branch dips below the rim of the pot

Cascade, a weatherbeaten old tree clinging to a cliff face. The foliage must fall below the base of the pot

Informal upright, with gently curving trunk

Broom, probably the most tree-like style for most of us with branches fanning out from the top of a straight trunk

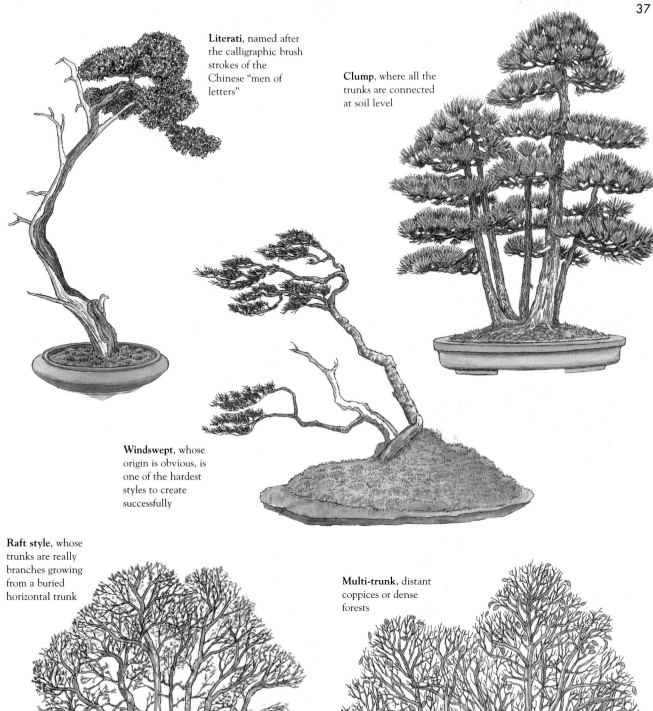

Literati, named after the calligraphic brush strokes of the Chinese "men of letters"

Clump, where all the trunks are connected at soil level

Windswept, whose origin is obvious, is one of the hardest styles to create successfully

Raft style, whose trunks are really branches growing from a buried horizontal trunk

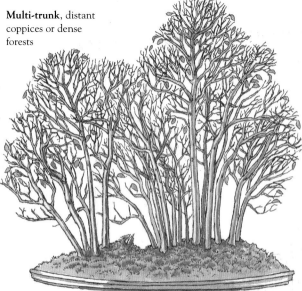

Multi-trunk, distant coppices or dense forests

TRIMMING TO SHAPE

YOUR FIRST TASK, probably within a few weeks of acquiring a bonsai, is to trim the new growth, and to pinch out buds in order to keep the tree looking neat. Hardy outdoor trees are dormant for four or five months a year, but tropical indoor trees can grow more or less constantly, although the lower light level in winter does slow their growth down a little.

The simple techniques are really just common sense, and are the same for both indoor and outdoor trees, but they do vary according to the way the different types of plant grow. For this purpose plants can be divided into six groups. The basic trimming techniques are outlined below. Variations are detailed in the Species Profiles where appropriate.

In spring and early summer, growth can be rapid and this is when regular trimming is needed to keep the bonsai in shape.

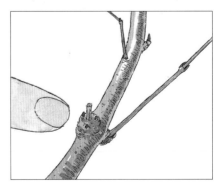

BROADLEAVED TREES

The leaves of broadleaved trees are flat and wide, like apple and oak, although they can vary enormously in size and shape. Some bear leaves in pairs, on either side of the stem, whereas others bear their leaves alternately, the first on one side, the next on the other side and so on. At the base of the stalk of each leaf is a tiny bud which is capable of growing into a new shoot.

Broadleaved trees with opposite foliage

Once the new shoot has one pair of leaves, you can pinch out the minute pair of emerging leaves in the center with tweezers. This will arrest the growth of that shoot and will prevent the remaining leaves from growing too large.

Longer shoots can be snipped back to just above a pair of leaves. Two new shoots will grow from where the leaves join the cut shoot, so bear this in mind when deciding how far back to cut.

Cutting a longer shoot at its base will induce many new, smaller ones to emerge from around the wound.

Broadleaved trees with alternate foliage

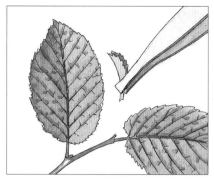

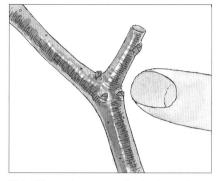

Once the shoot has two full-sized leaves, snip off the growing tip to stop it growing longer. A new shoot will soon emerge from the base of each leaf.

To build up a dense mass of twigs, let each shoot grow until it has five or six leaves and prune it back to one leaf. Not only will a shoot grow from the base of this leaf, but many new buds will form around the base of the shoot.

Trees with very small leaves can be trimmed almost like a hedge. But cut each shoot individually, *between the leaves*, not through them. Cut leaves turn brown and are ugly.

Spring-flowering trees

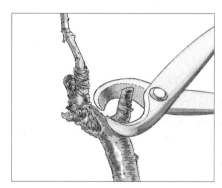

Flowering species, such as Japanese apricot, *Prunus mume*, are pruned to induce blossom rather than for shape.

Although the general shape of spring-flowering trees is important, the trimming technique is designed primarily to induce flowering.

As soon as flowering has finished, prune out any of last year's shoots which spoil the neat outline of the tree.

Any older spurs can also be thinned out at this time.

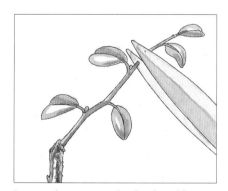

Let new shoots grow unhindered until late summer. Towards the base of each shoot, the buds are a little fatter or rounder. These are next year's flower buds. Prune back to allow two or three of these buds to remain.

This is a fairly advanced technique which should only be used on *healthy deciduous broadleaved trees*.

In early to midsummer, once the first crop of leaves has hardened, remove every leaf by cutting through its stalk. It is a good idea to prune the shoots at this time as described on pages 38–39.

Within a few weeks, new shoots will emerge from the base of every leaf stalk These bear fresher and smaller leaves.

Leaf pruning also improves the "twigginess" of the tree. Only use this technique in alternate years at the most; otherwise your bonsai may become exhausted by the extra effort of double the growth in one season.

PINES

Pines bear needles in groups of two, three or five, which do not initially have buds at the base. Pines do not easily produce buds on older wood which has shed its needles.

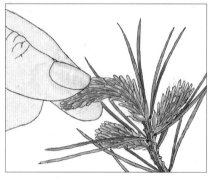

Pine shoots emerge like candles with tiny needles pressed closely to them. As the candles grow, the needles elongate and peel away from the shoot.

As the needles begin to peel away, pinch off the top one- to two-thirds of the shoot. New buds will form at the broken point for next year. Some buds will also form at the base of the shoot.

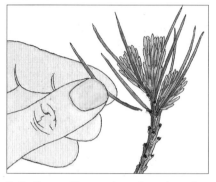

Pull off most of last year's needles to keep the tree neat.

Pines, like this Japanese white pine, can quickly become straggly if their growth is not kept in check by pinching and pruning.

Allowing the candle to develop fully and removing it all in late summer will encourage new buds to form further back down the branch.

JUNIPERS

Junipers either have scale-like leaves pressed close to the stem, or short needles born in whorls of three around the stem. Some have a combination of both types of foliage. Each needle or scale has the potential to form a bud at its base so that the foliage can become very dense and compact.

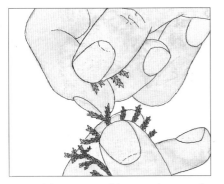

Tufts of dense juniper foliage can be gripped between the thumb and forefinger of one hand while the tips are simply pulled off.

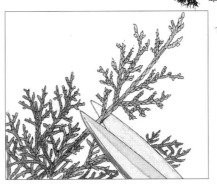

Extension shoots should be cut back almost to the base.

As the dense foliage of Chinese juniper grows, the tree appears to swell like an inflating balloon.

OTHER CONIFERS

All other conifers bear needle-like leaves singly, and only a few have buds at the base. Unlike pines, most will readily produce buds on older wood.

Allow the shoots to grow until the leaves begin to darken and snip the shoots back to keep the tree neat.

If no buds develop on the remaining part of the shoot, it can be removed completely the following spring. The buds which formed at its base will grow to replace it. Leave very short shoots unpruned.

Most conifers bud back well provided correct trimming procedures are observed.

REGENERATION PRUNING

This juniper has become too overgrown; the inner foliage has begun to die off and will need to be regenerated.

Pines and other conifers

Allow shoots to grow unhindered on branches you want to shorten and in late summer remove them completely. Make sure that you leave some old foliage on last year's growth.

Junipers

Cutting back the central "spine" of all branchlets will encourage tufts of new foliage to burst from branch intersections.

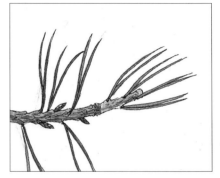

During the winter, and into the following summer, new buds will form back along the branch.

AFTER A FEW YEARS, the canopy of your bonsai may have grown too large in proportion to the trunk, or some branches may have become too long. To rectify this, you must first encourage new shoots further back along the branch, then you can prune back to those shoots and use them to rebuild the foliage mass.

Most deciduous hardy trees and broadleaved tropicals will throw out new shoots from old wood after very severe pruning, and respond well to having all foliage and buds pruned away. On the other hand, conifers demand that all branches have sufficient foliage to maintain sap flow, so they need to be pruned back in stages over a number of years. Pruning away all foliage on a conifer branch will almost certainly result in the death of that branch.

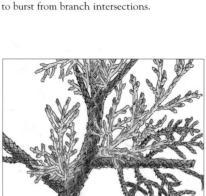

These take a year or two to grow long enough to use for replacement, but there will be so many of them that the tree will very quickly fill out again.

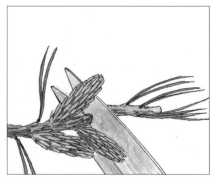

Once these buds have opened and the new shoots have begun to harden, you can prune back to them and use them to rebuild the foliage mass.

All broadleaved trees

If you examine the shoots and branches you will see evidence of dormant buds at old leaf scars or internodes, as well as at the point where branches fork.

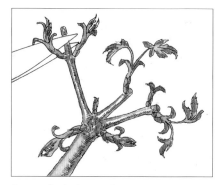

Pruning back close to these points in midsummer induces these buds to develop. Leave a short stub at first and remove it when the new shoots have hardened off.

If you are nervous about this, in midsummer cut all new shoots, in the area you want to regenerate, back to within a short distance of their base, leaving no foliage. New shoots will form at the base of the stub and further back down the branch. You can then carry out step two, above, next year.

PRUNING BRANCHES

Sometimes you may want to open up the canopy or change the overall shape by removing branches entirely. Don't be afraid to do this – it won't harm the tree. Current horticultural thinking recommends leaving a stub to protect the trunk against decay until the wound heals. This may be practical on fully grown trees, but it looks ugly on a bonsai.

Special tools for pruning bonsai are available from all specialist nurseries. Although they make life easier, they can be expensive and are by no means essential. If you have them, then use them, but this section assumes you will just be using common household tools.

1 Cut the branch as close to the trunk as possible with pruning shears or a keyhole saw.

2 Use a sharp modeling knife or gouge to pare the remaining stub of wood flush, and to hollow out its center a little.

3 Seal the wound, making especially sure to cover the edges where the cut bark is exposed. Non-drying children's modeling clay can be used (the kind that comes in many colors – mix a color to match the bark!). Or use grafting wax or bees' wax, both mixed with a little olive oil to stop it hardening completely. As the wound heals, the

bark rolls over the cut surface and pushes the soft sealer off automatically.

Never use bitumen paint or any wax that dries hard. The former will indelibly mark the bark and the latter will pull away live bark when you try to remove it.

REPOTTING AND ROOT PRUNING

THE VERY THOUGHT of this task fills most newcomers to bonsai with horror. But, far from being cruel, it actually benefits the plant by mimicking what would naturally take place in the wild. For example, if a wild oak's roots were allowed to grow freely each year, by the time it reached maturity they would stretch for a quarter of a mile in all directions! Forests could not exist because the roots of all the trees would strangle each other.

In fact, what happens is that each year the tree grows some new extension rootage, for anchorage and regeneration, and a lot of new, short-lived fine feeder roots. Most of these new roots eventually die when they become entangled with more vigorous roots from nearby trees, when they are eaten by subterranean wildlife, or when they have simply become too old. It is this constant regenerative process that keeps the roots, and therefore tree, in good health.

In pot culture, this process is interfered with. The roots are not subjected to the same conditions. They rapidly fill the pot until either they cease to function efficiently or they strangle themselves and die. This may sound as if it reproduces nature but it doesn't. Dead roots in a pot will decay, and because the total root length is comparatively short, the decay can reach right up to the trunk and the whole tree will consequently die. By repotting and root pruning your bonsai periodically, you will be doing it a favor, and it will reward you with increased health and vigor.

If you still need convincing, remember that, by using this technique, the Japanese have managed to keep potted trees alive and healthy for centuries!

When and how

The frequency of repotting depends largely on the species, size and the age of each individual tree, and more specific details are given in the Species Profile section. However, the technique is identical, regardless of any of these factors.

The best time to repot any tree is towards the end of the dormant season, just before the buds begin to swell. With tropical and subtropical trees, mid spring in your area is best. Even though there is no dormant season as such, the growth slows down in winter and surges again as the days lengthen in spring. Spring flowering apples and cherries should be repotted in early fall, and azaleas and quince immediately after they have finished flowering.

BONSAI SOIL

- Soil must provide stability for the plant, hold water and nutrients for the roots, and be sufficiently open to allow free passage of roots, water and air. It must also be free-draining.

- Most imports from Japan are growing in a special granular clay, unique to the Akadama region. Bonsai from other Far Eastern countries are generally planted in a more compact clay. These soils suit the trees in their native countries, but in our homes and yards they are not necessarily ideal.

- Japanese Akadama is widely available, and Japanese maples seem to prefer it. But I have grown Japanese maples in a good general-purpose bonsai soil for years with excellent results. All trees will grow sucessfully in it.

Basic recipe

3 parts of coarse peat, leaf mould or similar organic matter
2 parts of coarse sand or fine grit

Sift all ingredients to remove particles smaller than $1/16$ of an inch and larger than $1/4$ of an inch before mixing thoroughly.

The removal of fine particles ensures good drainage and air capacity, and provides the roots with easy access. The absence of coarse particles enables the soil to be worked in between the roots easily. Extra grit should be added for outdoor trees in rainy climates. Other variations are given in the Species Profiles section.

How to repot a tree

1 Carefully ease the tree from its pot. You should see a mass of roots coiled around the root ball. No roots may mean that the tree was pot-bound and they have begun to decay. Either way, the tree needs urgent repotting.

2 Use a knitting needle or something similar to untangle the long roots and to rake away some of the old soil. If the roots are healthy, remove about half the soil and leave the rest intact.

3 If the roots are not so healthy, remove all the soil. To avoid damage, use a hose or running faucet to wash the soil away. Standing the root ball in a bowl of water for ten minutes first will loosen the soil.

4 Remove all dead or decaying roots, cutting them back to healthy ones. Shorten the rest until the root ball will fit the pot with a clear margin of about an inch (25 mm) or so all around.

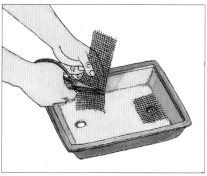

5 Wash the pot and cover the drainage holes with plastic mesh to stop the new soil falling through.

6 Place a thin layer of grit or small gravel in the base of the pot to aid drainage and cover this with a layer of fresh soil. Then make a small mound where the trunk will sit.

7 Position the tree in the pot, aligning the "front" correctly. Bonsai look best when they are positioned slightly off center. Bed the trunk into the mound of soil by twisting it gently back and forth. Hold the tree in place with wires or nylon string passed through the drainage holes and tied over the roots.

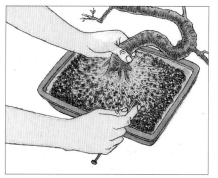

8 Add fresh soil, using the knitting needle to work it in well into all the spaces between the roots. This is much easier if the new soil is a little dry. Fill up with fresh soil to within ¼ inch or so from the rim to allow for watering. After a few weeks, the soil will settle and you can top it up with more.

9 Water thoroughly and keep the tree where it will be protected from frost, direct sun and wind until new growth has started. Don't water again until the soil has visibly begun to dry out a little, and then water sparingly until new growth is established. Don't feed until new growth is well under way.

SHAPING WITH WIRE

ONCE YOU HAVE lived with your new bonsai for a while, you may become dissatisfied with the shape or position of some of the branches, or you may want to train new branches into a certain position. Perhaps a straight branch would be improved by adding a curve or two, or a narrow fork would look better if it were widened.

Some books advocate using suspended weights, guy lines or

Scars caused by wire that has been left for too long take many years to heal and will never completely disappear. In severe cases, the branch may die.

Selective pruning and careful wiring of all twigs and shoots can produce a fine, open, and balanced structure like this Chinese juniper.

Ideally, each branch and foliage mass should occupy its own clearly defined area, with space between it and its neighbors.

Even newly made *jins* (dead branches) can be positioned with wire and will set in place as the wood dries out.

Some branches are too thick to wire and are best left alone. Attempting to bend them might cause damage to the bark or worse.

other contrivances. However, these are all inaccurate and inefficient and usually a waste of time. By using the technique described below, branches can be shaped and positioned with precision.

Aluminum wire is the kindest to the bark because it is soft. It is available from all specialist bonsai dealers in many sizes. Some garden or hardware stores also stock a limited range. Copper wire is also good, and is used exclusively for conifers in Japan. It can be salvaged from pieces of electrical cable, and it can be annealed (softened) by heating it and then allowing it to cool slowly. Once used, it hardens through use and holds the branch firmly. Practice the technique on a twig of similar size from a garden shrub until you get the hang of it.

Before you begin, decide where you want to position the branch or

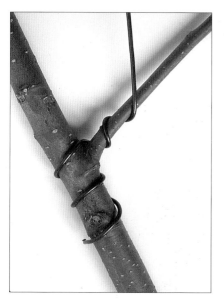

Starting to wire a branch.

Wiring two branches with one piece of wire.

Wiring a fork.

introduce the curves. Select a piece of wire one-third longer than the branch, and thick enough to hold the branch in position. If you gently test the resistance to the branch and compare it to the wire a few times, you will soon be able to judge if the wire is strong enough to hold the branch in position.

1 Anchor one end of the wire by coiling it around the trunk or main branch. Continue coiling the wire around the branch at about a 45° angle.

2 The branch and wire together can then be gently maneuvered into position. As the tree grows, a new layer of wood is laid down beneath the bark. (This is what causes the annual rings you see in the end-grain of a block of wood.) This new wood grows to the new shape of the branch and will eventually hold it in position.

3 Check carefully once a week for signs of the wire cutting into the bark. As soon as you see this beginning to happen, remove the wire immediately. Using wire cutters to cut it off is safer than trying to unwind it. The branch may already have set. If not, reapply the wire, but this time coil it in the opposite direction to the first application. This is kinder to the bark and less likely to interrupt the flow of sap.

Young, vigorous branches on broadleaved trees can set in a matter of weeks, while others take longer. For example, junipers can take years, and several applications of wire are necessary.

HOW TO WIRE A BRANCH CORRECTLY

- If the wire is too tight, it will damage the bark.

- If it is too loose, the wire will not hold the branch in position.

- Ideally, the wire should barely be in contact with the bark.

- If one wire isn't sufficient to hold the branch, apply another parallel to the first, *never* crossing, as this will create pressure points that will scar the bark.

CHAPTER FOUR

PESTS AND DISEASES

*Although bonsai are no more susceptible to insect
pests than any other plants, they are less able to
defend themselves than full-sized trees because
their growth is so slow. In nature, a tree would
be able to put on new growth at a much faster
rate than even a major infestation could
devour or destroy it – this is its natural
method of defence.*

*The same applies to fungal infections and
diseases, which can spread at an alarming rate,
especially when a bonsai is in the cosy
environs of the average living room
or in its protective winter quarters.*

IDENTIFYING AND TREATING PROBLEMS

THE CONDITIONS THAT protect the bonsai tree from damage by the elements also favor the rapid development of diseases. However, once diagnosed, most pests and diseases are easily eliminated with ordinary garden chemicals.

Prevention

As with human diseases, prevention is better than cure, and good plant hygiene is the first precaution. Remove all affected foliage from the tree and the surface of the soil, and isolate diseased trees from the rest of your collection.

A monthly dose of general garden insecticide and fungicide (not at the same time) should be routine. Use "systemics" whenever possible. A systemic fungicide or insecticide is one that is absorbed into the plant and carried in the sap until it reaches all parts of the plant and remains there until it gradually breaks down. Not only does it rectify any existing problem, but it protects the plant against future attacks for a while. The information on the package will tell you how long the treatment lasts. Systemics can be applied by spraying onto the foliage or by watering into the soil.

Diagnosis and Treatment

• The crucial thing is to be vigilant. Each day, as you water your trees, inspect them for telltale signs.
• When spray-treating the foliage, add a drop of household detergent to the mix. This will help the droplets adhere to shiny leaves, and helps it penetrate the waxy protective coating some insects produce.

TAKING CARE WITH CHEMICALS

• All garden chemicals are potentially dangerous. Always follow the manufacturer's instructions exactly and avoid breathing in any spray. Wash hands thoroughly after use and dispose of surplus chemicals by diluting and then burying them. Never pour them down the drain.

• Never use systemics on Chinese elm *(Ulmus parvifolia)*. This species dislikes them for some reason, and tends to lose its foliage and some young, soft shoots.

Premature yellowing of the foliage usually indicates a problem with the roots. The roots of this bonsai willow are rotting through lack of aeration.

DISCOLORED FOLIAGE

Yellow leaves

Evergreen trees shed their leaves from time to time, as they become old and are replaced by new ones. The older leaves will turn yellow shortly before they fall. Provided that it is only the older leaves that are affected, there is nothing to worry about.

Yellowing of younger leaves can be a symptom of general poor health caused through too dry roots, cold or drafty conditions or insufficient feeding. All these should be considered as possible causes and rectified if necessary.

Some APHIDS and SCALE INSECTS, which feed by sucking the sap from tender young stems, can cause the leaves to yellow as they are deprived of nutrition. Treat with an appropriate insecticide.

Black blotches

There are a number of microscopic BLACK SPOT fungi which cause this symptom. The fungi, although unsightly, are not fatal to plants grown outdoors. However, when plants are protected, the disease can spread rapidly without the wind and rain to disperse the spores. The resulting defoliation, as heavily infected leaves wither and fall, is more dangerous to the plant than the disease itself. Remove all affected foliage and treat with an appropriate fungicide.

LEFT
Sap-sucking aphids puncture the tissue of young shoots, causing distortion to the new leaves and debilitating the tree.

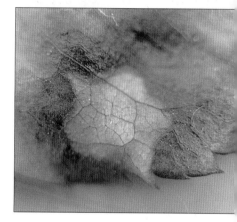

BELOW
Black spot fungi cause unsightly disfiguration of affected leaves and spread rapidly to other parts of the plant.

Powdery white deposit

This is invariably powdery mildew, which is a common garden fungal disease. It thrives on plants with poor air circulation around the leaves and roots which are constantly on the dry side. Treat with mild fungicide and improve the growing conditions to prevent the infection reoccurring.

Powdery mildew is a fungal disease attracted by poor air circulation and dry roots.

DRY, PAPERY PATCHES

The occasional, roughly circular patches are probably caused by the hot sun shining through water droplets, which act like tiny magnifying glasses. Avoid watering or spraying in full sun.

Dry margins to the leaves indicate that they are losing water too rapidly, either because the tree is receiving too much direct sun or because it is exposed to too much wind – warm or cold. Consider choosing another place for the tree.

Irregular ribbons of dried tissue are caused through LEAF MINERS, which burrow under the surface of the leaf as they feed. They are harmless and only affect the occasional leaf. No treatment is necessary.

WILTING LEAVES

Although a sudden increase in temperature, or drying of the surrounding air can cause wilting, this is nearly always a sign of a root-related problem. Dry roots are the most obvious cause, so check this first. Ironically, overwatering can also cause foliage to wilt. Constantly wet roots literally drown and begin to rot. Without healthy roots to absorb moisture, the tree can suffer from drought. Review your watering schedule.

If your watering schedule is not to blame, then the most likely cause is VINE WEEVIL grubs. The "evil weevil" is responsible for more untimely deaths of container-grown plants than any other single cause. The wingless adult beetle is harmless, merely nibbling at the edges of leaves, especially rhododendrons. But the voracious

Leaf miners burrow under the surface of the leaf as they feed and leave papery trails in their wake.

larvae live in the soil where they devour roots at an incredible rate. By the time the symptoms are apparent, it is often too late to save the tree. Lift the tree from its pot and check the roots. If you see no vine weevils, gently tease away the soil and hunt for the larvae, destroying any that you find. Keep going until all the exposed roots are healthy. If you have found no larvae by then, the cause of the wilting is probably one of the physiological ones mentioned above. Either way, replace the tree in its pot and add fresh soil as required

There is no effective chemical treatment for vine weevil available to the amateur gardener. However,

If you find vine weevils – panic! Treat your entire collection with parasitic nematodes.

in recent years, a biological control has become available. Tiny parasitic nematodes can be introduced to the soil. They will seek out and kill any larvae that exist at the time, and remain active for about three weeks. In practice, an application every two months or so is sufficient. If you have trouble finding these nematodes, try a specialist organic gardening supplier.

It is important to be especially observant when repotting. Any telltale tunnels in the soil should be investigated further.

Dry leaves and premature defoliation are signs that something is wrong and closer inspection is urgently required to diagnose and rectify the problem.

DISTORTED LEAVES

Several fungi, such as PEACH LEAF CURL, cause leaves to become swollen and distorted. The infection generally starts on established leaves and works its way to the growing tip of the shoot. Once established, the disease is difficult to cure, but commercial treatments are available from gardening suppliers. To prevent infection, treat all bonsai of the prunus family as soon as the leaves have begun to harden as a matter of routine.

When distorted leaves emerge from the buds, the cause is probably tiny APHIDS which suck sap from the growing tips of the shoots, where the tissue is thin and easily punctured. Treat with an appropriate insecticide.

TOP
Various fungi cause distortion of the foliage, like this peach-leaf curl. Systemic fungicides keep it at bay, but total eradication is difficult.

ABOVE
In spring, ants carry their herds of aphids to the tender growing tips, and "milk" them to feed the young ants. An infestation like this can eventually kill the growing shoot.

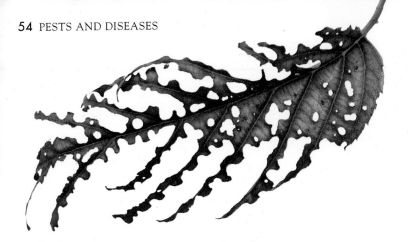

RAGGED LEAVES

Many insects nibble away at leaves, but none of them are particularly dangerous in small numbers. The general rule of thumb is that if you can see them, destroy them; if you can't, they have probably gone away. Standard preventative treatment should prevent further damage.

The one exception is when you see regular, "U"-shaped notches around the leaf margins. This could be a sign of adult vine weevils, so treat the soil against the larvae for at least the next three months. These adult vine weevils feed at night, so grab your flashlight and start hunting for them!

AREAS OF DRIED FOLIAGE

Where there are localized areas of dry leaves which seem reluctant to fall, there are probably SPIDER MITES as well. These almost microscopic little devils enjoy dense foliage, where they are protected from rain or overhead watering. They live on sap, and form large colonies which kill the adjacent leaves. Although not spiders at all, they do produce

web-like filaments to hold these dead leaves in place, thus adding further protection and enabling them to multiply and spread further. If you shake the affected area over a sheet of paper, you should see minute black specks appear as the dead mites fall. Remove all dead foliage and spray the affected area with a jet of very cold water. Treat with an appropriate insecticide at regular intervals until the symptoms disappear.

Another possible cause is damage to the bark and underlying tissue further back along the branch. Some insects will "ring-bark" a twig, but these are all itinerant and there is no appropriate treatment. It is more likely that the branch has been partially snapped by accident or that wire has been left on for too long and is restricting the sap flow.

The adult vine weevil (above) is wingless and climbs the tree at night to feed on the leaves. It is harmless in itself, but its grubs are the most feared of all pests (see page 53).

Itinerant leaf-eaters, spiders, short-sighted birds, and the ravages of the weather all take their toll on leaves. By the end of the summer, the foliage of many bonsai is past its best – that's nature!

FLUFFY WHITE DEPOSITS

Take a close look; some of these can be smaller than a pinhead, and may appear relatively insignificant.

On pines, ADELGIDS produce waxy protective fibers at the base of needles, particularly on young shoots and around the buds. The colonies build up very rapidly and can eventually kill the shoot if it is not treated. Treat with an appropriate insecticide: watering into the soil and spraying the affected areas. Add a drop of household detergent to the spray to help the liquid penetrate the waxy coating.

Some APHIDS also produce a sweet, waxy substance which protects them as well as feeds the ants! Treat as above.

SCALE INSECTS vary in size from ¼ of an inch right down to ⅟₅₀ of an

LEFT
Adelgids infest pine shoots and protect themselves with a sticky, waxy, fibrous coating. A little detergent in the insecticide spray will help it penetrate.

BELOW LEFT
Scale insects are like tiny limpets, sometimes only a millimeter across. They can be picked off by hand, but a systemic insecticide is a more effective treatment.

inch. They have shallow, conical, brownish shells – very much like limpets. They raise these shells during damp weather, or when they are on the move, and expose the fluffy, white protective fibers underneath. They are difficult to remove by hand and multiply rapidly. A severe infestation can kill the affected shoot. Contact insecticides have very little effect, even with added detergent. Treat with three applications of an appropriate systemic insecticide at intervals recommended by the manufacturer. The first will kill the adults but not the eggs and the subsequent applications will take care of any new hatchlings.

Finally, from time to time, little bonsai toadstools may appear in the pot. The vast majority are harmless, if they are dangerous, the tree would have been showing symptoms of root decay for some time. In fact, many trees actually benefit from the presence of certain fungi in the soil, which break down the nutrients into a readily digestible form. If they are large and unsightly, pull them out. If they are in proportion with the tree, leave them and enjoy the added bonus.

Microscopic gall mites live and breed inside the leaves of many species, causing a variety of swellings and pimples which are harmless but nevertheless disfiguring.

SPECIES PROFILES

This Species Profiles section has been prepared with the beginner very much in mind and includes the 50 species most commonly used by commercial bonsai producers. It provides useful background information to help you understand your bonsai a little better, and lists all the specific horticultural requirements, as well as providing tips on training and general care. It is worth referring to this section before you buy a bonsai, so you can be aware of each species' needs.

Each entry in the Species Profiles gives you an insight into the natural habitat and climatic conditions of the particular species. This can help you understand your bonsai – why some tropicals dislike too much sun, why some trees insist on having their roots frozen, and why a change in watering regime induces specific reactions.

It also includes details of each species' idiosyncrasies such as brittle branches, delicate bark, etc., so you don't have to learn the hard way! There is nothing worse than lovingly wiring a branch only to find that it snaps off at the base as soon as you start to move it; or carefully trimming every shoot, and then watching them all die back.

Every plant needs its own combination of soil, sun, water, and feed. Deviating too far from the correct amount of any of these will cause the tree to sulk and may even initiate more serious physiological problems which could permanently – even fatally – affect its health. Not only is it important to know what these requirements are, but it is equally important to understand why. There will be times when you will have to use your own judgement, and a sound horticultural knowledge of the plant is essential. All this information is provided in the text and is also encapsulated in an "at-a-glance" chart for quick and easy reference.

CHART SYMBOLS

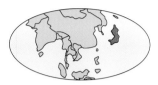

Bonsai sources

The map shows you where your bonsai is likely to have been produced, while the text tells you where the species is found in the wild.

Light levels

Sunlight through a window has different properties to natural sunlight. A plant that likes sun outdoors may not appreciate a sunny windowsill indoors. The symbols show where to site your bonsai, inside or outside, while the text tells you if and how this would be varied.

 Full sun outside

 Dappled shade or full afternoon shade outside

 Shade outside

 Full light inside, but away from hot afternoon sun

 Shaded inside

✓ Tick indicates preferred light level

°F -10 0 10 20 30 40 50 60 70 80 90 100

Temperature range

Here, the thermometer displays the range within which your bonsai can be kept with absolute safety. However, since the weather is never entirely predictable, it is useful to know how far each species' tolerance can be stretched, and the text supplies this information.

Pests and diseases

All plants play host to a variety of insects and fungal infections. Most are either harmless, invisible, or both, although a few are fatal. This section lists the most common pests likely to attack each species.

Soil

Bonsai trees have specific soil requirements in order to maintain the delicate balance of air, water, and nutrients, made more difficult by the shallow container. Although the "standard mix" is suitable for most species, many will perform better with certain variations.

Watering

It is so easy to kill a tree through over-watering, even with the best of intentions. Similarly, insufficient water can kill some trees alarmingly quickly. The symbols will show you at a glance how the watering regime varies from season to season, and the text gives more specific advice.

 Water generously once soil has begun to dry a little

 Keep the soil well moistened but avoid over-watering

 Keep the soil damp but not wet

Feeding

The three main nutrients each play specific roles in healthy growth. Varying their proportions as well as the quantity and frequency of feeding, in the right way, not only keeps the plant healthy but can also induce specific reactions. The symbols show instantly the ideal feeding regime, while the text supplies further details.

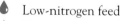 Balanced feed

 Low-nitrogen feed

 Nitrogen-free feed

Pruning

Pruning is carried out at different times of year in order to achieve specific results. Here the more detailed information in the main text is distilled to provide an easily accessible guide for quick reference.

ACER BUERGERIANUM

Trident maple

HARDY

A SMALL, ELEGANT tree originating from eastern China and Japan. Although full-size trees are rarely seen in the West, trident maples are a common roadside and parkland tree in the Far East. Mature trees may have a fissured and scaly bark, but when grown as bonsai, the bark remains a delightful pinkish gray with occasional flaking patches.

Trident maple bonsai are invariably imported from Japan and generally fall into three categories – large, heavy-trunked specimens; root-over-rock styles; young, slender-trunked group plantings.

The heavy-trunked specimens are produced by growing the tree in open ground for many years until a sufficient trunk girth is achieved. At this point, all the branches are removed and the trunk is shortened to the desired height. New branches grow rapidly from around the wounds, and are trained to shape immediately.

One of the most endearing factors of this species is that it will tolerate extremely severe root pruning, which makes it ideal for bonsai cultivation. When the stumps are dug from the ground, the roots are pruned back to within a few inches of the trunk base, and immediately regenerate to form the network of fine roots necessary for life in a pot.

Root-over-rock styles also take advantage of the trident maple's vigorous root system. When the roots are wrapped tightly around a rock, their rapid growth ensures quick results. Furthermore, the rock tends to absorb heat from the sun during the day and this warmth encourages the roots to thicken much quicker than they would under normal conditions, thus producing good heavy roots which are in proportion to the trunk.

The triple-trunk style is executed almost perfectly in this specimen trident maple. The well-spaced branches create an illusion of great size and maturity. A lot can be learned from just looking at bonsai trees like this!

Although it is healthy enough, this attempt at a root-over-stock style will never succeed. The single, thin root makes the tree appear precarious rather than strengthening the composition. Look for a better example than this.

The smaller, younger trunks lean away from the "parent" tree to reach the light. Following the natural habits of full sized trees creates a very believable image, which can add considerable value to a bonsai.

Young plants are often planted in groups. The bushy growth creates a dense canopy which can be trimmed like a hedge to produce a convincing miniature forest.

What to look for

When buying heavy-trunked or root-over-rock trident maples, examine the trunk for ugly scars or stumps of old branches, and avoid trees which have either. They are usually stocked in large numbers, so you will always be able to find a better one. Group plantings should have trunks of varying thicknesses and heights to add realism and perspective to the composition.

Points to watch

The thick, fleshy roots of trident maples contain a lot of water. Although this species is hardy, prolonged freezing of waterlogged roots can cause them to "explode" when the water inside them expands as it freezes. Ensure that the soil – and the roots – are kept just moist, but not wet, during the winter. Put the tree in a shed or garage to prevent the soil becoming waterlogged by winter rain.

ACER BUERGERIANUM

BONSAI SOURCES

Japan.

LIGHT LEVELS

OUTSIDE   INSIDE

Full sun or partial shade.
Small trees should have the pots shaded to avoid overheating the roots. Warm, drying winds may cause leaf margins to scorch.

TEMPERATURE RANGE

°F -10 0 10 20 30 40 50 60 70 80 90 100

Tolerates freezing for brief periods. Protect from severe freezing by placing in an unheated shed or garage.

PESTS AND DISEASES

Generally pest-free. Occasional aphid attacks. Powdery mildew results from dry roots and poor air circulation around foliage.

SOIL

ORGANIC 60%	GRIT 40%

Japanese Akadama clay is excellent. Repot annually. Roots may be cut back hard if necessary.

WATERING

SPRING	SUMMER	FALL	WINTER
💧💧💧	💧💧💧	💧💧	💧

Water well during growing season, but keep soil just moist during the winter.

FEEDING

SPRING	SUMMER	FALL	WINTER
💧	💧	💧	

Balanced general-purpose feed during growing season, substituted by nitrogen-free feed in late summer/fall.

PRUNING

Late winter for main branches. Constant trimming of new shoots during growing season. Pruning weak branches by a third in midsummer will encourage rapid extension growth and strengthen the branch.

ACER PALMATUM

Japanese maple

HARDY

THIS SPECIES IS the queen of bonsai. Originating from Japan, its small, delicate, five- to seven-lobed leaves and fine twigs produce truly elegant shapes. It responds well to all bonsai training techniques by issuing new buds from all parts of the branches and forming compact, fibrous root systems. Wounds heal rapidly and the young branches are flexible but readily set in position after wiring.

There are many strains used in commercial bonsai production, most of them unnamed. The spring leaves emerge from copper-color through orange to deep red, maturing to various shades of green, often with red or orange margins. In fall, they turn bright orange to deep crimson.

Because of their popularity, Japanese maple bonsai are produced in vast quantities. Sizes vary from tiny "starter" trees to large, very expensive masterpieces. However, because of a preference for the species' feminine appearance, the more rugged styles like root-over-rock are seldom seen.

The willingness of Japanese maples to throw out adventitious shoots from old wood has its disadvantages as well as advantages. You will often find long, straight shoots growing vigorously from towards the center of the tree. If allowed to grow unchecked, these can drain the energy from the finer twigs that form the tree's outline. Shorter spurs will also grow from branch intersections in large numbers. These can cause the canopy to become too dense and cluttered, which reduces ventilation

The trunk arrangement here is almost perfect. Perspective is created by using trunks of different sizes and placing the smaller ones to the rear and sides of the composition. The shallow container enhances the graceful appearance of this bonsai.

LEFT
This fairly typical, medium-priced maple has an interesting trunk, but the branches and twigs have been allowed to grow out of proportion. Reducing the bulk by about a third would be an improvement. A good buy.

and makes the plant vulnerable to fungal infections. Lack of light in these dense areas can also cause some valuable branches to die back.

The answer is to ensure that all unwanted growth is removed as soon as it is noticed. As your bonsai matures, some of the older twigs should be pruned away and the area rebuilt with some of the many new young shoots that will appear.

Japanese maples are woodland trees and prefer dappled shade. Full sun may exhaust the tree by midsummer.

What to look for

Unfortunately, large-scale commercial production means that many Japanese maple bonsai offered for sale have very severe and often ugly pruning wounds, with clusters of branches emerging from the same point. This looks unnatural, and should be avoided unless you are sure you can disguise the wound by carving. Buy only group or forest plantings, when the trees are in leaf, so you can be sure that all trees are the same strain.

Points to watch

The delicate leaves are easily scorched by hot sun and, more easily, by drying winds. Protect from both at all times. Various types of aphids colonize the growing shoots of Japanese maples. These can be difficult to spot as they tend to adopt the same color as the shoot on which they are feeding. Cold winds in winter can kill some of the very fine twigs produced during the previous summer.

ACER PALMATUM

BONSAI SOURCES

Japan. Home-grown bonsai are produced in some western countries, but rarely with the same skill as even the largest Japanese nurseries.

LIGHT LEVELS

OUTSIDE · INSIDE

Partial shade at all times.

TEMPERATURE RANGE

°F -10 0 10 20 30 40 50 60 70 80 90 100

Tolerates freezing for a week or so at a time. In really severe cold spells, place in a shed or garage until the weather improves. Constant summer temperatures over 86°F may cause the plant to "shut down" but will not damage it permanently.

PESTS AND DISEASES

Aphids are common but easily controlled. Occasional spider mite infestations. Powdery mildew kills young shoots if air circulation is poor and roots are allowed to become dry.

SOIL

ORGANIC	GRIT
60%	40%

Japanese Akadama clay is excellent. Repot annually for smaller trees; every three years for larger and older bonsai.

WATERING

SPRING	SUMMER	FALL	WINTER
💧💧	💧💧	💧💧	💧

Keep soil evenly moist throughout the year. Never allow it to become bone dry. Avoid watering during the hottest part of the day.

FEEDING

SPRING	SUMMER	FALL	WINTER
💧	💧	💧	

Balanced general-purpose feed from spring to late summer. Nitrogen-free feed from late summer through fall.

PRUNING

Late winter for main branches. Trim new growth to shape and thin as necessary during growing season.

ACER PALMATUM
'DESHOJO' OR 'CHISHIO'

Japanese red maples
HARDY

THESE TWO SIMILAR varieties are true red maples, unlike the inferior *atropurpureum*, which has large, dull, burgundy-colored leaves and coarse growth, and is not suitable for bonsai cultivation.

Red maples have small, neat leaves borne on short red shoots which emerge from pale gray twigs. In spring, the leaves are bright red and gradually darken to reddish-green in summer. They are very susceptible to wind and sun scorch, so must be protected from both. However, too much shade will cause the leaves to lose most of the red color as the chlorophyll content is increased to compensate for the low light levels. Whenever I exhibit my chishio indoors, even for just a few days, the reduced light level causes the leaves to become entirely green and remain that color for the rest of the season.

The answer is to place the bonsai where it is shaded from direct sun by a tall tree or building, but where it receives full "sky light" from above. If your red maple does lose its color, you can remove all the foliage by cutting through the leaf stalks (petioles) in midsummer. Within a week or two, a fresh crop of leaves will emerge. They will be smaller, borne on shorter shoots, and will have full red coloring. Provided the tree continues to receive good

This specimen was originally collected from open ground, and utilizes the natural clump formation. The wide, open, and airy crown is typical of the tree in nature.

overhead light, this color will darken slightly and remain until fall. This leaf-pruning should only be carried out on healthy trees, and only in alternate years at the most.

In fall, the leaves turn bright orange to crimson, the colors being richer on foliage that has not suffered from scorch or on trees that have been leaf-pruned earlier in the growing season.

Red maples are slow-growing, so in order to create recognizable tree forms in a relatively short time, commercial growers tend to produce two- or three-trunked styles more often than with other species.

What to look for

For single-trunked trees, follow the advice given for Japanese maples (page 61). When choosing multi-trunked styles, select a tree whose trunks vary in thickness. The thickest should be the tallest, the thinnest should be shorter and positioned towards the back to enhance the perspective. Trunks should join at the very bottom, not

The foliage on this specimen deshojo maple is now beginning to adopt its greener summer hue. If leaf pruned, a fresh crop of bright red leaves will appear, which should remain that color for the remainder of the season.

part-way up the main trunk and, because the slow growth also slows the healing process, trunks should be free of ugly wounds.

Points to watch

Leaves are delicate and easily damaged by wind, sun, drought, and insect attack. If the soil is allowed to remain too dry, these problems are exaggerated, and some shoots may be lost. Frequent pruning back to the same point will promote knotty clusters of small shoots which must be thinned to two or three in order to maintain an elegant branch line.

Trees that have come into leaf while under plastic or glass must be slowly acclimatized before being permanently placed outside, to prevent leaf scorch.

ACER PALMATUM 'DESHOJO'/'CHISHIO'

BONSAI SOURCES

Japan.

LIGHT LEVELS

OUTSIDE   INSIDE

Semi-shade.
Avoid direct sun except in the early morning, but ensure good overhead light to maintain color.

TEMPERATURE RANGE

°F -10 0 10 20 30 40 50 60 70 80 90 100

Temperatures constantly over 86°F will cause the tree to cease growing, but will do no permanent harm. Tolerates freezing for short periods. Place plants in an insulated shed or garage in really severe cold weather.

PESTS AND DISEASES

Red aphids are difficult to spot – look for telltale distorted young shoots. Powdery mildew may occur where air circulation is poor.

SOIL

ORGANIC	GRIT
60%	**40%**

Japanese Akadama clay is excellent. Repot every one to three years. Annually for smaller trees and every three years or so for older and larger specimens.

WATERING

SPRING	SUMMER	FALL	WINTER
💧💧	💧💧	💧💧	💧

Keep evenly moist throughout the year. Protect from continuous rain in the winter.

FEEDING

SPRING	SUMMER	FALL	WINTER
💧	💧	💧	

Weak balanced feed spring and summer. Nitrogen-free feed from late summer through fall. Too much nitrogen will cause the leaves to turn green.

PRUNING

Late winter for major branches and thinning out older twigs. Trim for shape during growing season.

ACER PALMATUM 'KIYOHIME'

Kiyohime maple

HARDY

THIS VARIETY OF Japanese maple is extremely slow-growing, forming little more than a low, spreading shrub in maturity. Because it is so slow-growing, specimen bonsai are rare and expensive, but smaller bonsai are more readily available.

In common with most new plant varieties, kiyohime maples are more delicate than others of the species and require a little more attention and disciplined approach to their upkeep. They are more easily scorched by sun or wind, they react more to dry roots or over-watering, and are less able to defend themselves against insect or fungal attack than their larger cousins.

The major idiosyncrasy of this variety is that, unlike most plants whose energy is channelled vertically, the kiyohime channels its energy horizontally. This means that if the upward growing tip, or apex, is pruned out or broken accidentally, it is very difficult to replace. The plant will content itself with growing sideways and will leave a hole in the top of the foliage canopy. For this reason, and because of its unusually dense and twiggy growth, most kiyohime are trained in the "broom" style, where all the branches radiate from the same point at the top of a clear, straight trunk. Indeed, it is almost impossible to train it in any other style.

If not regularly thinned by pruning out older twigs and allowing new shoots to replace them (not at the apex!), the canopy will become too congested. The ends of many

The natural horizontal growth pattern of this species is clearly utilized in this specimen. Only the side branches must be pruned. Any attempt to prune the few upward-growing branches would result in total loss of the central part of the crown, and would ruin the bonsai for ever.

The classical "broom" style is typical of a well-developed kiyohime maple bonsai. The trunk will thicken later on.

This typical commercial "starter" bonsai is already beginning to display the characteristics of kiyohime maple. Careful pruning and wiring will eventually produce a fine bonsai every bit as good as the specimen opposite.

ACER PALMATUM 'KIYOHIME'

BONSAI SOURCES

Japan.

LIGHT LEVELS

OUTSIDE   INSIDE

Semi-shade.
Protect from direct sunlight, but ensure unimpeded exposure to overhead "sky-light."

TEMPERATURE RANGE

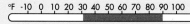

Foliage may dry out if kept above 86°F for too long. Will withstand a degree or two of frost for short periods. Larger bonsai are tougher.

PESTS AND DISEASES

Aphids, spider mites, and small caterpillars of various kinds enjoy the protection that the dense foliage provides. Powdery mildew and occasional black spot fungi can be a problem.

SOIL

ORGANIC	GRIT
60%	**40%**

Japanese Akadama clay is excellent. Repot every two years.

WATERING

SPRING	SUMMER	FALL	WINTER
🌢🌢🌢	🌢🌢	🌢🌢	🌢

Keep evenly moist throughout the year. Never allow soil to dry out.

FEEDING

SPRING	SUMMER	FALL	WINTER
🌢	🌢	🌢	

Gentle, balanced fertilizer from late spring to late summer, nitrogen-free from late summer to fall.

PRUNING

Little branch pruning should be necessary. A regime of regular trimming to shape and annual thinning of cluttered, dense twigs should be rigidly observed. Do not prune the central leader.

---

branches will die back through lack of light and air. Trim and thin regularly throughout the growing season to maintain shape and a balanced, open canopy.

In spite of all these drawbacks, kiyohime make fine and highly prized bonsai if properly cared for.

What to look for

Most importantly, don't buy any kiyohime maple that doesn't have a healthy, growing apex or central part of the canopy. Choose a plant that has a good, straight trunk with evenly distributed, radial roots and an evenly formed framework of branches. Lopsided plants will rarely develop into good, well-balanced bonsai even in expert hands.

Points to watch

Protect from wind and direct sunlight during summer and store in an unheated but insulated shed or garage in winter. Don't overfeed or overwater and never let the roots become dry. Take special care when working on the apex of the tree.

ACER PALMATUM
'SEIGEN'

Seigen maple
HARDY

ARGUABLY THE MOST prized of all Japanese maples, the main attraction of this rare variety is its coloration. The buds open with tiny, bright red leaves that soon turn deep coral pink as they expand, maturing to mid-green edged with orange-red. In fall, healthy foliage turns bright crimson. This annual symphony of color is beautifully reflected in the pale gray bark, which seems to adopt vague tints of the foliage.

Seigen maples are pretty rare but, because of their desirability, a lot of the examples exported from Japan are somewhat inferior in quality. In order to satisfy the high demand, producers are forced to export trees that would not meet the aesthetic standards required of other varieties. So if you do acquire a seigen maple, expect to have to do a lot of work on it. You may have to do some surgery on the upper trunk to create taper, and be prepared to build the branches up from nothing. It seems unreasonable to have to do this on an expensive plant, but the result is well worth it.

Seigen suffer from wind scorch and dry roots. Although the tree itself is very tough and resilient, the foliage is more delicate and easily damaged. Color can be improved by ensuring good light and by avoiding high-nitrogen fertilizers.

The spectacular spring color temporarily compensates for the sometimes odd-shaped trunks of commercial seigen maples. The naturally elegant twigs and foliage also suit this more flowing style.

Photographed just as the new leaves emerge following summer leaf pruning. If you look carefully at the trunk, you can see how the tree has been pruned over the years to develop this realistic form.

What to look for

When selecting a seigen maple, look first at the surface root formation. Choose one which has a natural-looking, radial root system that curves gently away from the trunk. The lower trunk should have a pleasant, gently curved shape, free of large scars. Because trees are produced rapidly, they are grown vigorously for a number of years and then pruned back hard, so the upper trunks tend to be scarred. Consider whether you could disguise or improve the scars by further pruning or carving.

Points to watch

The delicate foliage must be protected from wind and direct sun. The ideal summer situation is a few yards away from the northeast side of a tall building or tree, where it will be shaded from all but early morning sun, but where the overhead "sky light" is unobstructed. Do not allow the soil to become waterlogged during wet winters. Place in a shed or garage to protect against excessive rain and prolonged freezing conditions.

ACER PALMATUM 'SEIGEN'

BONSAI SOURCES

Japan.

LIGHT LEVELS

Semi-shade.
Good overhead light will improve the color; direct sun will destroy the leaves.

TEMPERATURE RANGE

°F -10 0 10 20 30 40 50 60 70 80 90 100

Tolerates freezing for short periods. Protect from prolonged or severe freezing by placing the tree in a shed or garage.

PESTS AND DISEASES

Aphids and occasional small caterpillars are the only real dangers. Powdery mildew or black spot fungi quickly appear on poorly ventilated or unhealthy trees.

SOIL

ORGANIC 60%	GRIT 40%

Japanese Akadama clay is excellent. Repot every one to three years. Larger or older trees require repotting less often.

WATERING

SPRING	SUMMER	FALL	WINTER
🌢🌢	🌢🌢	🌢🌢	🌢

Keep evenly moist throughout the year. This variety can be very thirsty in summer.

FEEDING

SPRING	SUMMER	FALL	WINTER
🌢	🌢	🌢	

Gentle, balanced feed during spring and early summer. Nitrogen-free fertilizer from late summer until leaf fall.

PRUNING

 Late winter for main branches. Pruning main branches in midsummer will promote strong vigorous new shoots which can be used to build new branch structures. Trim to shape during growing season and thin congested areas in late winter.

ARUNDINARIA AND SIMILAR SPECIES

Bamboos
HALF-HARDY

This is fairly typical of many ornamental bamboo imported from China. It is hardly a bonsai, but it is a start!

PROBABLY THE SPECIES with the most oriental flavor, but seldom used as a subject for specimen bonsai in the East, except for large group plantings on flat slabs, which imitate naturally occurring groves. More commonly, bamboos are cultivated for accent plantings which are used to accompany larger specimen bonsai of other species when displayed in the traditional Japanese tokanoma.

In the West, bamboos are more popular as bonsai in their own right, mainly because of their curiosity value. Although nearly all bamboos can survive in open ground in temperate climates, they do not overwinter so well in pots, and should be treated as half-hardy.

Bamboos are a form of grass with hollow, woody stems. The leaves grow from internodes which are regularly spaced along the stem, and from the growing tip of each

stem. Pinching out the soft tip of each stem with tweezers will encourage smaller leaves to emerge on short shoots from internodes further down the stem. Eventually these shoots will become too bushy and un-bamboo-like. At this point, the stems should be cut away at the base. They will be replaced with new stems that regularly sprout from the fleshy roots throughout the growing season.

When removing stems, aim for a tall, graceful, open composition, with smaller and younger stems towards the rear and sides, larger ones at the front. New shoots growing from the roots should be removed as soon as they are noticed if they are likely to spoil the composition.

BELOW
This magnificent bamboo grove is planted on a natural slate. It is seen here on display at the 10th International Bonsai Exhibition in Osaka, Japan.

Bamboos prefer a constant supply of moisture, but will not tolerate a waterlogged soil. Ideally, they should be watered twice a day in hot, dry weather.

Bamboos can be kept indoors all year round provided that the air is not too dry, although they prefer to be placed in fresh air in summer.

What to look for

Choose a variety that has small, neat leaves of uniform size. Inspect the base of each stem carefully. When bamboos have been kept in the same soil for too long, the roots become congested and more easily waterlogged. This causes the bases of the stems to rot, which deprives the already weakened roots of sugars and can easily kill them.

Points to watch

If your bonsai grove begins to weaken, the cause will probably be either congested roots or a too large stem draining energy from the others. If the roots are congested, transplant into a larger temporary container until next repotting season, when roots can be pruned or the plant divided. Don't be afraid to cut oversized stems away at the base – this will give the rest of the plant a new lease of life.

ARUNDINARIA

BONSAI SOURCES

Southeast Asia, mostly China and Japan.

LIGHT LEVELS

OUTSIDE   INSIDE

Full sun or partial shade.

TEMPERATURE RANGE

°F -10 0 10 20 30 40 50 60 70 80 90 100

Tolerates high temperatures provided humidity can be maintained. Minimum winter temperatures 40°F.

PESTS AND DISEASES

Root rot may affect waterlogged plants. Scale insects can rapidly colonize stems and spider mites may occasionally infest clusters of small shoots at internodes.

SOIL

ORGANIC	GRIT
80%	**20%**

Repot every two to three years. Either replant in a larger container or cut the root mass into clumps; and replace half in the same pot and use the rest in the garden or for growing more bonsai.

WATERING

SPRING	SUMMER	FALL	WINTER
🌢🌢🌢	🌢🌢🌢	🌢🌢	🌢

Water frequently during hot weather, but avoid waterlogging. Reduce water during winter, but never allow to become drier than moist.

FEEDING

SPRING	SUMMER	FALL	WINTER
🌢	🌢	🌢	

Balanced feed throughout spring and summer. A dose of nitrogen-free fertilizer will toughen plants not being overwintered indoors.

PRUNING

Cut away old, large stems at the base from early spring to late summer.

BOUGAINVILLEA

TENDER

A SUBTROPICAL, semi-evergreen climber of the southern hemisphere, most commonly from South America. The many varieties of bougainvillea are now usually grown as garden climbers throughout the subtropics in both hemispheres and are a familiar sight adorning Mediterranean villas.

The main attraction of this species – either as a garden plant or as a bonsai – are its showy, highly colored bracts which surround the rather less significant flowers. Varying from pure white through pinks to crimson, these bracts are often mistaken for petals, whose function they also perform, although they are more durable.

In nature, bougainvillea has a straggly growth, but older plants develop a thick trunk base if all suckers (growth emerging from roots or trunk base) are removed as soon as they appear. These thick trunks are harvested to be trained as bonsai and, because of the time involved, the final product can be expensive. Smaller, less well-developed examples do become available at a reasonable price, however, but rarely will they ever develop into larger trees when confined to pots.

Most climbing plants start life in the shade of taller trees, where their roots are shaded, and grow upwards so their leaves and flowers

Truly magnificent specimen bougainvillea bonsai like this are very rare and highly prized. Nevertheless, this was once just a stump with a few young shoots.

are exposed to the sun. For this reason, bougainvillea bonsai do best when they are able to receive good light but when their roots are kept reasonably insulated from the heat. A deeper-than-normal container and plenty of *fibrous* organic matter helps achieve this. Too much fine organic matter will retain excessive

moisture which can easily cause roots to decay.

In winter, keep the plant in a light, but not sunny, position where the temperature is maintained above 45°F, and allow the soil to become almost dry, maintaining it at this level until growth starts in spring. Prolonged periods of too cool

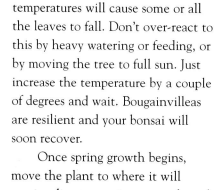

temperatures will cause some or all the leaves to fall. Don't over-react to this by heavy watering or feeding, or by moving the tree to full sun. Just increase the temperature by a couple of degrees and wait. Bougainvilleas are resilient and your bonsai will soon recover.

Once spring growth begins, move the plant to where it will receive direct morning sun and good overhead light for the rest of the day. Increase water at this time so that the soil becomes evenly moist but never waterlogged.

What to look for

If you can afford a large specimen the most important thing to look for is an interesting, unscarred trunk with no old wire marks on the main branches. Subsidiary branches can be pruned and replaced.

Smaller bougainvilleas are best grown as full- or semi-cascades, or literati (long-trunked) styles. The large leaves and bracts are not suitable for more normal tree-like shapes. If buying bougainvillea during the colder months, avoid any plant that has lost its leaves, or which is not firm in its pot (an indication of root decay).

Points to watch

In temperate zones, bougainvilleas may be kept outdoors after acclimatization. A too rapid change of environment may cause foliage loss and retard flowering. Insufficient light, too much or too little water will also deter flowering and the production of the accompanying colorful bracts.

BOUGAINVILLEA

BONSAI SOURCES

Most bonsai produced in China, Korea, Singapore, and Indonesia; also some in the Mediterranean region, Central America, and United States.

LIGHT LEVELS

 OUTSIDE INSIDE

Good light in winter, away from direct sun. Lighter position in growing season with full morning sun.

TEMPERATURE RANGE

°F -10 0 10 20 30 40 50 60 70 80 90 100

Minimum 45°F for short periods; ideally keep temperatures in winter above 54°F. As hot as you like in summer, provided roots are cool.

PESTS AND DISEASES

Generally pest-free. Powdery mildew may affect plants kept indoors if ventilation is poor. Root aphids and vine weevil can cause problems, so inspect roots regularly.

SOIL

FIBROUS ORGANIC 70%	GRIT 30%

Keep soil open and free-draining. Deeper containers and naturally fine roots mean that repotting is only necessary every three to five years or so. Remove as much of the old soil as possible.

WATERING

SPRING	SUMMER	FALL	WINTER
💧💧	💧💧	💧💧	💧

Almost dry in winter, evenly moist in summer. Never saturate the soil.

FEEDING

SPRING	SUMMER	FALL	WINTER
💧	💧	💧	

Low-nitrogen feed during growing season. Chelated iron may improve color of bracts.

PRUNING

Prune current season's growth immediately after flowering, in early fall. Major branch pruning, if necessary, can be carried out during the winter.

CARMONA MICROPHYLLA

Fukien tea
TENDER

LEFT
A typical example of the many thousands of commercial *Carmona* bonsai exported to the West from China each year. The trunk and the root spread are already showing signs of the fine specimen that will develop in time.

A tapered trunk with gentle curves and an interesting root formation make this specimen of *Carmona* highly desirable.

ALSO KNOWN AS *Ehretia buxifolia*, this large evergreen shrub can be covered in masses of tiny white flowers all year round if sufficiently high temperatures and humidity can be provided. It is commonly used as a garden and hedging shrub throughout Southeast Asia, although most commercial bonsai originate from southern China.

The shiny, dark green leaves are borne densely from buds which burst through the buff to brown bark on all parts of the tree. In fact, there are so many shoots that almost any shape can be achieved simply by pruning back to a leaf which is facing in the direction you want the new shoot or branch to grow. A new shoot will emerge from the base of the leaf stalk. All unwanted shoots and buds should be removed as soon as they appear so that all the energy is channeled into the desired parts of the tree.

Fukien teas can be kept indoors all year round, but on hot summer days they will enjoy some fresh air, provided that they are not introduced to full sun before they have become acclimatized. To do this, place the tree in the sunshine for an hour during the early morning on the first day. Increase the time by half an hour a day until the leaves have become fully hardened. Too sudden exposure to full sun will quickly dry out the leaves and debilitate the plant.

If kept indoors during the summer, make sure that your bonsai doesn't receive full sun through a window after mid-morning.

Sudden drops in temperatures, which are common in temperate climates, will cause yellowing and subsequent loss of foliage.

To encourage flowering, maintain temperatures between 68–86°F and spray with tepid water several times a day. Standing the pot in a tray of wet gravel will help maintain local humidity.

What to look for

Choose a plant with an interesting trunk or, in group plantings, with a good variety of thicknesses. The branch structure is not so important because you can easily prune off all existing branches and grow a new set in a very short time. Leaves should be dark and glossy. Flowers should be evenly distributed all over the tree. Localized flowering can be a symptom of stress or poor health.

Points to watch

The dense habit of Fukien tea means that you will have to clean unwanted shoots from the trunk and main branches several times a year in order to maintain the tree-like appearance. Foliage pads can be trimmed like a hedge for a year or so but will then need to be thinned to allow light and air to penetrate. Fukien tea will die if exposed to even a light frost, so maintain winter temperatures well above freezing to be safe.

Masses of small, shiny leaves form dense foliage clouds which need regular trimming and thinning to maintain good health. When temperatures are kept between 68–86°F, and high humidity is maintained, carmonas will produce masses of tiny white flowers all year round.

CARMONA MICROPHYLLA

BONSAI SOURCES

Mainly from southern China.

LIGHT LEVELS

OUTSIDE INSIDE

Full sun outside.
Protect from full direct sun indoors after mid-morning.

TEMPERATURE RANGE

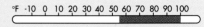

°F -10 0 10 20 30 40 50 60 70 80 90 100

54–95°F. Hotter temperatures will not harm the tree if the air humidity is high.

PESTS AND DISEASES

Aphids, spider mites, and scale insects all love Fukien tea. Add a little detergent to sprays to help the droplets adhere to the glossy leaves. Powdery mildew and occasional black spot might occur.

SOIL

ORGANIC 80%	GRIT 20%

Repot every two to three years. Do not feed until growth has restarted, and keep soil just moist, not wet, for two weeks after repotting. This encourages new roots to grow in search of water.

WATERING

SPRING	SUMMER	FALL	WINTER

Keep soil wet in growing season and well moistened (but not waterlogged) when growth is slower.

FEEDING

SPRING	SUMMER	FALL	WINTER

Low-nitrogen feed all year round when winter temperatures are high. Reduce feeding in winter if growth slows down at this time. Too much nitrogen will reduce flowering.

PRUNING

Branch pruning and trimming can be done at any time.

CARPINUS SPECIES

Hornbeams

HARDY

THE TWO SPECIES used for commercial bonsai cultivation are *Carpinus laxiflora* – Japanese hornbeam and *Carpinus turczaninowii* – Korean hornbeam. Bonsai of both species are produced almost exclusively in Japan.

Both hornbeams have smallish, neat leaves and fine twigs, and both will respond well to pruning by producing new shoots from around the wound. Care should be taken when training with wire because the branches and twigs seem supple at first but have a habit of snapping suddenly if bent too far.

The Japanese hornbeam has pointed, mid-green leaves with serrated margins. Leaves turn golden yellow in fall. In older trees, the pale gray bark develops paler gray, interconnected streaks running from the roots upwards almost to the apex. This creates an extremely attractive, ancient yet elegant bonsai. Smaller trees can develop this pattern if they are grown rapidly at first and then restricted in pots for a number of years. Forest plantings of slender Japanese hornbeams with two-tone trunks are highly desirable, but because they can be produced very easily, they are not too expensive.

Korean hornbeams have smaller, rounder leaves and slightly finer twigs. The bark is dark gray,

Hornbeams are generally grown in this natural style that echoes a classic parkland tree. This specimen has an excellent trunk and branch placement.

sometimes with a mahogany tint, but remains smooth until it is very old. The bonus is that, in fall, Korean hornbeams turn a brilliant orange – one of the few species to do so, and almost unique in bonsai.

If you are lucky, your hornbeam might produce masses of yellow-green catkins. To encourage this, keep in full sun and dose with low nitrogen feed such as tomato or rose fertilizer.

All hornbeams suffer from wind scorch, even in cool, wet weather, but are quite tolerant of full sun.

What to look for

Most commercial hornbeam bonsai are good quality, whether groups or single trees. Although the foliage canopy may seem healthy and dense, further inspection might reveal a lot of dead twigs and branches which are hidden beneath the leaves. Satisfy yourself that the branch structure would still be acceptable when these have been removed before committing yourself.

Points to watch

Inner branches and twigs can die back through lack of light and air if not regularly thinned and pruned. Keep the finer twig structure open by trimming all new shoots to one or two leaves and removing all larger leaves as they appear. In late winter, thin out the twigs to leave only the shorter, finer ones, and to maintain a "breathing" space between the major branches.

CARPINUS SPECIES

BONSAI SOURCES

Japan.

LIGHT LEVELS

OUTSIDE   INSIDE

Full sun or semi-shade.
Shade pots of trees kept in full sun to prevent them overheating.

TEMPERATURE RANGE

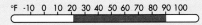
°F -10 0 10 20 30 40 50 60 70 80 90 100

Tolerates freezing for up to a week or so at a time, providing the tree is not exposed to drying winds. Protection against temperatures below 22°F or light freezing for more than a week is advisable.

PESTS AND DISEASES

 Generally pest-free. Localized aphid attacks. Itinerant leaf-nibblers may take chunks out of the odd leaf. Mildew can occur when growing conditions are poor. Small toadstools are the fruiting bodies of a symbiotic fungus that helps the tree absorb nutrients.

SOIL

 ORGANIC **60%**   GRIT **40%**

Repot every two years.

WATERING

SPRING SUMMER FALL WINTER

Water well during the growing season and don't allow the soil to become even slightly dry. Maintain very moist during winter.

FEEDING

SPRING SUMMER FALL WINTER

Balanced feed from spring to midsummer, followed by nitrogen-free until leaf fall. Replace balanced feed with low-nitrogen feed to induce flowering.

PRUNING

Trim new shoots to one or two leaves during summer. Further thinning of shoots and branch pruning in late winter or early spring, before buds open.

CELTIS SINENSIS

Chinese hackberry

HARDY

A SMALL DECIDUOUS tree with shiny, oval leaves. The spring flowers are insignificant, but the small, bright orange fruits are attractive, if a little reluctant to set. Although this species is fully hardy, it is often sold as an indoor bonsai, probably because it is commercially produced in China, where nearly all half-hardy and tender bonsai come from.

Having said this, it is perfectly happy when kept inside, provided that the conditions are right. First, it must receive good light. Second, because it is deciduous, it must be given a dormant period. Outdoors, this occurs naturally, but indoors you must create these conditions artificially. If you have a balcony or outside windowsill which is sheltered from the wind, then this would be the ideal situation. Failing this, a north-facing (south-facing in the southern hemisphere) inside windowsill where the window can be opened during the day will suffice. If the tree is not allowed to have a proper rest period during winter, it will quickly become exhausted and will die before the next spring.

Whether kept indoors or out, hackberry prefers really hot summers, which encourage more prolific fruiting. It also likes a humid atmosphere and plenty of moisture in the soil.

Growth can be very rapid. If shoots are allowed to grow until they bear eight to ten leaves, and are then cut right back to one or two leaves, a mass of smaller shoots will develop from around the wound and back along the branch. These will quickly form a dense canopy of fine twigs. Bear in mind that as the network of twigs becomes more dense, the flowers and fruit will become fewer. It is up to you to decide whether you prefer a finely developed tree form or a less tree-like but attractive, fruit-bearing bonsai. After a year or two you will be able to find the right balance.

What to look for

Nursery *Celtis* are trimmed regularly, so they often have fine twigs, many of which die back to leave large gaps. Make sure that your bonsai has not suffered from this problem.

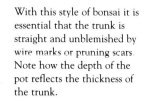

With this style of bonsai it is essential that the trunk is straight and unblemished by wire marks or pruning scars. Note how the depth of the pot reflects the thickness of the trunk.

Points to watch

Celtis likes lots of water in the growing season and will quickly wilt and shed leaves at the first sign of dry roots. It will also suffer from root rot if the soil remains too wet, especially when the tree is not growing strongly or during the dormant season.

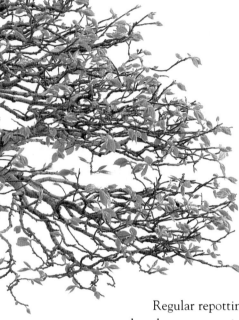

The well-structured branches support an even, fine tracery of twigs. A good example of the "broom" style.

Regular repotting will ensure that the roots remain healthy. Using a deeper than normal container will help. Shading only the pots from full sun in really hot weather or when placed on a sunny windowsill, will aid water retention and keep roots in good condition.

CELTIS SINENSIS

BONSAI SOURCES

China.

LIGHT LEVELS

OUTSIDE · INSIDE

Full sun.
Shade pots, but not foliage, from really hot sun.

TEMPERATURE RANGE

°F -10 0 10 20 30 40 50 60 70 80 90 100

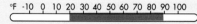

Minimum 25°F. Will tolerate freezing for a week or so at a time. Place in an insulated shed or garage during longer spells of severe cold.

PESTS AND DISEASES

 Scale insects and spider mites are the main enemies. Aphids are rare. Many microscopic fungi can cause small blotches on leaves, but they are harmless and easily eliminated by removing and destroying affected leaves.

SOIL

ORGANIC	GRIT
60%	**40%**

Repot annually.

WATERING

SPRING	SUMMER	FALL	WINTER
🌢🌢	🌢🌢🌢	🌢🌢	🌢

Water well during the growing season and keep fairly moist in the dormant season.

FEEDING

SPRING	SUMMER	FALL	WINTER
🌢	🌢	🌢	

Low nitrogen during spring and summer. Nitrogen-free from late summer to leaf fall.

PRUNING

Trim to shape regularly during growing period. Prune branches and thin over-dense twigs in late winter/early spring.

CHAENOMELES

Flowering quince

HARDY

The ample pot provides a good reservoir for moisture which is needed in larger amounts while the tree is producing flowers.

A COMMON GARDEN shrub found in temperate zones throughout the world, valued for its prolific flowering on older branches and spurs during late winter and early spring, before the leaves have emerged. The variety normally used for commercial bonsai production is *Chaenomeles speciosa*, from Japan, which has small glossy, mid-green leaves and small bright crimson flowers with yellow centers.

Flowering quinces are medium-sized shrubs which spread by producing suckers (new shoots which grow from the spreading roots). Rather than trying to prevent this from happening, commercial growers and bonsai masters alike use selected suckers to produce clump-style bonsai. The suckers are regularly pruned hard to encourage flowering and to create interesting shapes in the trunks. The constant removal of the unwanted suckers also promotes equally interesting shapes in the main roots. These are frequently exposed by raising the plant in its container, creating the impression of a riverside tree, whose roots have been exposed as the bank has been eroded away.

Smaller bonsai are sold as single stem styles, but are better if allowed to develop into clumps.

Because of the necessity to prune entirely to promote flowering,

quince are regarded as "single-season" bonsai. But the season is a long one – my quince normally begins flowering before Christmas (in the UK) and is still bearing blossom in May. To prune for flowers, cut younger twigs back to two buds immediately that part of the tree has finished flowering. (Each part of the tree is living on its own share of the root system, so

pruning one part of the tree has little effect on other parts.) Allow new shoots to grow unhindered until late summer. When the bark of these new shoots begins to harden off and change to a buff-brown color, prune the shoots back to two to three buds. These buds will

The different colored blossoms on this specimen Japanese quince are the result of grafting several varieties onto the same rootstock. The trunks have sharp angles, caused by regular hard pruning.

develop into flowering spurs during the next few years.

The small, hard, yellow fruits are attractive, if a little too large in proportion to the tree. If left in large numbers, they can exhaust a tree in a small container, so they should be removed before they fully develop. You can leave three or four, if you like, but bear in mind that they grow tight to the branch, and removal of ripe fruits often causes damage to the spur.

What to look for

Try to buy your quince when it is in flower. Some strains have larger flowers that might be out of proportion to the tree. The leaf size is unimportant. The trunks should have interesting shapes containing many sharp bends. Straight trunks are a sign of immature, mass-produced trees.

Points to watch

If too many suckers are allowed to grow freely, they will drain energy from the older parts of the tree and retard flowering. Prune suckers right back, cutting into the old wood. Leaving a stub will encourage more suckers to grow from its base. Quince are thirsty and wilt at the first sign of dry roots. Entire branches may be lost if not watered immediately.

CHAENOMELES

BONSAI SOURCES

Japan.

LIGHT LEVELS

OUTSIDE   INSIDE

Full sun if pots can be watered frequently; otherwise semi-shade.

TEMPERATURE RANGE

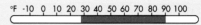
°F -10 0 10 20 30 40 50 60 70 80 90 100

Tolerates freezing for a week or so at a time. Early flowering can be induced by keeping frost-free.

PESTS AND DISEASES

Aphids and scale insects are common. Some caterpillars also enjoy quince. Mildew often attacks young crowded shoots. Cankers can occur on older wood – cut back to healthy wood immediately.

SOIL

ORGANIC 70%	GRIT 30%

Repot annually in fall or immediately after flowering. Do not feed for three weeks after spring repotting. Raise plant in its pot to expose surface roots.

WATERING

SPRING	SUMMER	FALL	WINTER
💧💧💧	💧💧💧	💧💧	💧

Plenty of water during summer; keep moist in winter.

FEEDING

SPRING	SUMMER	FALL	WINTER
💧	💧	💧	

Low-nitrogen feed during spring and early summer; nitrogen-free from midsummer to fall.

PRUNING

Prune to shape immediately after flowering. Leave new shoots unpruned until late summer, then cut back hard.

CHAMAECYPARIS OBTUSA

Hinoki cypress

HARDY

HINOKI CYPRESS is a popular subject for bonsai, but can sometimes be difficult to find. It has flat, fan-like sprays of evergreen foliage, with tiny, scale-like leaves pressed close to the shoot. The mid-green leaves are edged with silver-blue, and the tips of the shoots curl downward slightly. Good specimen hinoki bonsai are highly prized in Japan, where they are often used for forest plantings as well as for single-tree styles. Exported hinoki are generally small and rounded, which is not their shape in nature. Authentic, conical specimens can be found, but are far more expensive because of the species' slow rate of growth.

Hinoki cypress have very dense foliage, which makes maintenance of established shapes relatively easy. Simply hold a cluster of shoot ends between thumb and forefinger of one hand and literally pull off all the tips with the other. This technique will ensure neat and even foliage clouds. The one drawback is that hinoki cannot be relied upon to grow shoots from old wood to use as replacement growth. Therefore, in order to maintain the size and shape of your bonsai, you should clean out all the dead leaves and debris from the underside of the branches to allow air and light to penetrate, while pinching new shoots hard back above. The combination of the two will encourage small shoots to grow at minor branch intersections.

Conifers look best – and remain in better health – when there is a generous space between branches. This allows ample light to reach the inner foliage, without which it would eventually die.

In common with all hardy cypresses, hinoki do not tolerate drought, and have developed a waxy coating to the leaves to conserve moisture. Allowing the pot to dry out or exposing a bonsai with frozen roots to drying wind can be fatal. The trouble is that, because of the protective waxy coating, it may take weeks, or even months, for the dead foliage to dry out and actually look dead! You may discover that you have been caring for a dead tree for a while, so be especially careful to ensure that the pot never becomes drier than moist.

LEFT
This very old cypress has developed a rounded crown over the years. Notice how well the inner branches of the tree have been cleaned of dead foliage.

ABOVE
Trunks of different widths and heights make this recently planted group worth buying. With care it will eventually make a fine specimen bonsai.

What to look for

Many small, cheap hinoki bonsai are little more than rooted cuttings, relying on their dense foliage for visual appeal. Look for an example with a thick trunk and attractive surface roots. Ensure that the trunk continues right through the canopy to the apex of the tree, and that the branches or potential branches are evenly distributed – not all coming from the same point.

Points to watch

Be especially careful when wiring hinoki cypress. The fans of new, foliage-bearing shoots are attached to the branch in a strange and precarious way, and are *very* easily dislodged. Many a newcomer to this species has meticulously wired an important branch, only to find most of the foliage on the floor! Spraying with clean water once or twice a day in summer keeps it in good health. Hinoki do *not* like being indoors, even for short periods.

CHAMAECYPARIS OBTUSA

BONSAI SOURCES

Japan.

LIGHT LEVELS

OUTSIDE   INSIDE

Semi-shade.
If exposed to full sun, ensure pots are well watered and shaded.

TEMPERATURE RANGE

°F -10 0 10 20 30 40 50 60 70 80 90 100

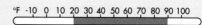

Tolerates freezing well. Protect from wind at all times.

PESTS AND DISEASES

Fungal attacks are rare. Red spider mites love the dry, protected environment of the dense inner branches, and can soon kill off large areas of foliage if not tackled quickly.

SOIL

ORGANIC 60%	GRIT 40%

Japanese Akadama clay can also be used. Repot every two to five years, depending on size, in mid-spring.

WATERING

SPRING	SUMMER	FALL	WINTER

Water well during growing season, keep moist in winter. *Never* let soil become even slightly dry.

FEEDING

SPRING	SUMMER	FALL	WINTER

Half-strength balanced feed from spring to fall. Top up with a nitrogen-free feed in late fall.

PRUNING

Prune during summer, when wounds will heal quickly. Pinch out growing tips as necessary.

COTONEASTER

Cotoneaster

HARDY

Cotoneasters grow vigorously in all directions and need constant trimming and pruning, as this example shows. The trunk has elegant curves which form an excellent base on which to build neat foliage clouds.

ORIGINALLY FROM CHINA, the many varieties of cotoneaster are some of the most popular garden shrubs in temperate and subtropical zones, and it is, without doubt, the ideal species for the newcomer to bonsai. The two varieties commonly used for bonsai are *Cotoneaster horizontalis*, and *C. microphyllus*.

C. *horizontalis* is a semi-evergreen, meaning that in mild winters it will retain some of its leaves – either green or in their attractive deep red fall color, but it is fully deciduous in colder weather or in poor conditions. Its tiny, mid-green leaves are glossy, and borne densely along either side of straight shoots. New shoots emerge from the base of every leaf stalk in midsummer or the following spring, creating the familiar "herringbone" growth pattern. The small pink flowers, which never fully open, are followed by masses of bright red berries which can remain on the plant well into winter.

C. *microphyllus* has a similar growth pattern, but is fully evergreen and has slightly longer, darker leaves. Its small, white flowers open fully in late spring, but they tend to set fewer berries than C. *horizontalis*.

Cotoneaster bonsai come in all shapes and sizes, so you should have no trouble choosing one that suits your taste, and once you have it there will never be a dull moment. Apart from the delightful seasonal changes in leaf color, flowers, and fruit, the regular and totally predictable growth pattern means that you can shape existing or new branches with little or no wiring, simply by cutting back to a leaf

facing the direction you want the new growth to take.

You will be forever snipping off the many unwanted shoots which will spring out from all parts of the tree throughout the growing season. The foliage clouds become so dense that you will need to thin them out by cutting away clusters of older twigs in order to allow younger ones to replace them. This may be necessary twice, or even three times a year. After a year or two of this frantic activity, you will be rewarded as you witness an almost perfect miniature tree developing before your eyes.

What to look for

Cotoneasters are slow to thicken in pots, so choose a specimen with an already well-developed trunk and surface roots. If the branches are not just right, you can always grow new ones within a couple of years. Any trees with weak trunks or thin, wayward roots should be avoided. Check that the roots are healthy and holding the tree firm in its pot.

Points to watch

All cotoneasters hate having wet feet and are often used to stabilize dry banks in gardens. It is crucially important to ensure that the soil used is free-draining and that overhead protection can be given during prolonged wet weather. Trunks and branches are very slow to thicken on container-grown plants. If you want to thicken the trunk on your bonsai, plant it in open ground or in a larger container for a year or two.

This cotoneaster was grown in open ground for many years after the roots were wrapped around the rock, to allow them to thicken. Once exposed to the air, they will hardly thicken at all. The gently cascading lower right-hand branch creates a very elegant bonsai.

The trunks of cotoneasters thicken slowly when grown in containers. It is important not to allow the bulk of the tree to become so heavy that it is disproportionate to the trunk.

COTONEASTER

BONSAI SOURCES

Japan.

LIGHT LEVELS

OUTSIDE   INSIDE

Full sun.
Can be kept indoors for periods in spring or summer.

TEMPERATURE RANGE

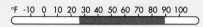

°F -10 0 10 20 30 40 50 60 70 80 90 100

Tolerates freezing, but does not like cold winds.

PESTS AND DISEASES

 Occasional aphid or red spider mite attacks are easily dealt with. Although rare on bonsai, fireblight fungus may attack flowers in some areas. It is incurable and usually fatal. Sterilizing all tools with a flame before and after use on cotoneaster is advisable.

SOIL

ORGANIC 50%	GRIT 50%

Repot every one to two years.

WATERING

SPRING	SUMMER	FALL	WINTER
🌢🌢	🌢🌢	🌢	🌢

Allow to become almost dry between waterings while growing and to remain barely moist in winter.

FEEDING

SPRING	SUMMER	FALL	WINTER
🌢	🌢	🌢	

Balanced feed in spring and summer. Nitrogen-free in late summer and fall.

PRUNING

Major branch removal in late winter/early spring. Trim and thin shoots constantly.

CRASSULA

Jade tree/Money tree

HALF-HARDY/TENDER

THERE ARE MANY varieties of *Crassula*, ranging from tiny ground-hugging types to the 10 feet tall *C. arborescens*, which is the variety most commonly used for bonsai. Not a tree at all, this species is really a succulent which originates from the South African Cape Province. It is a plant of semi-desert areas, so is able to thrive in the hottest temperatures, yet is unaffected by the low night temperatures that occur in deserts. It can even withstand a light frost.

Ironically, this species is one of the best for the newcomer, with no knowledge of horticulture, to use in order to learn how plants grow and respond to pruning. Provided the roots are not allowed to become too wet, *Crassula* are virtually indestructible. The growth pattern is uniform – leaves are borne in pairs, at regular intervals, and at right angles to the previous pair. A dormant bud is visible at the base of each fleshy leaf, and this will always produce a new shoot when the branch is pruned back to that point. Harder pruning will always induce the production of shoots from clearly visible internodes (old leaf scars) on older parts of the plant.

By using these attributes, a convincing tree shape can easily be built by even the most nervous of beginners, without wiring and

This specimen *Crassula* is quite old, and has been shaped entirely by selective pruning over a period of many years.

without any of the problems associated with older, more horticulturally temperamental species. The experience and confidence gained through this exercise will encourage budding enthusiasts to tackle more challenging projects in the future.

The worst enemy of *Crassula* is water. Its roots are not able to

defend themselves against decay if they are constantly wet. The plant may appear totally healthy until, one day, it just falls over. But even if this should happen , all is not lost – your obliging *Crassula* will readily take root again if the following procedure is observed:

• Cut away the rotting base of the trunk, so no decaying tissue remains.

Regular hard pruning of the upward-growing shoots of this clump style will encourage stronger side growth which can be developed into branches.

• Allow the wound to dry out for a few days, until the edges begin to curl inward as the tissue shrinks.
• Plant the trunk like a giant cutting in a mixture of about 20% organic matter and 80% grit, burying it deep enough to hold it upright.
• Maintain the soil barely moist until new growth is well under way. *Crassula* put out roots in dry conditions in order to find water, whereas other species only take root if water is already present.

What to look for
Most *Crassula* sold as bonsai are very small and untrained, so provided you make sure the roots are in good condition and the soil is free-draining, the world is your oyster!

Points to watch
Although *Crassula* can withstand the occasional light frost, don't assume that all examples will be equally tough. If the soil is wet *and* too cold, it could mean trouble. If the leaves begin to wrinkle, the plant has become too dry.

CRASSULA

BONSAI SOURCES
China, Taiwan

LIGHT LEVELS

OUTSIDE   INSIDE

Unconditional full sun.
Will tolerate semi-shade.

TEMPERATURE RANGE
°F -10 0 10 20 30 40 50 60 70 80 90 100
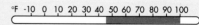

Minimum 41°F. Will withstand occasional *light* frost if soil is not wet.

PESTS AND DISEASES

Scale insects adore the juicy stems. Insecticides are not so effective on crassula, so remove these by hand.

SOIL

ORGANIC 30%	GRIT 70%

Fine grit is best. Free-draining, loam-based soil mixes can be used but require less water. Repot just before spring every two to three years. Keep warm and slightly dry for three weeks.

WATERING

SPRING	SUMMER	FALL	WINTER

Allow soil to become *almost* dry before watering, and to remain *almost* dry during winter.

FEEDING

SPRING	SUMMER	FALL	WINTER

Half-strength balanced feed while in active growth.

PRUNING

Pinch growing tips as necessary to maintain shape. Prune branches any time while tree is in active growth.

CRYPTOMERIA JAPONICA

Japanese cedar

HARDY

THIS UNIQUE SPECIES is the Japanese answer to the massive Californian redwoods. It has red-brown, stringy bark, and rich blue-green, pointed foliage. In Japan, this tree grows to an immense height and provides wonderful, red, decay-resistant timber.

Specimen bonsai of the species are highly prized and are therefore rare and expensive, but small- to medium-sized bonsai of the dwarf cultivar, *C.j. yatsubusa*, are produced in quantity in Japan. The short needles clothe the stout green shoots so densely that they almost completely hide them. Adventitious shoots grow prolifically from branch intersections and from old internodes on branches and trunks.

The application of wire to branches can be hampered by the dense growth, and the branches, although apparently flexible, can suddenly snap if bent too far. Once the wire has been applied, bend the branch just a little at first, increasing the bend by small amounts every three to four weeks until the desired position is reached.

The foliage can be kept neat by simply nipping out the growing tips of each shoot with the fingernail and thumbnails. This repeated process will stimulate vast numbers of new shoots to grow from within the foliage cloud, causing congestion

which might eventually cause the dieback of parts of the branch. To avoid this, the older twigs must be periodically pruned out so that younger shoots can grow on to replace them. The comparatively open foliage clouds will quickly fill out again.

As old foliage dies naturally, it can collect in the forks of the fine twigs, creating the ideal habitat for red spider mites, which will eagerly start to weaken and eventually kill

that part of the tree. It is essential that all dead foliage is regularly cleaned out, allowing light, air and, more importantly, water to penetrate the inner areas. Regular spraying with clean, cold water not only deters red spider mite, but imitates the natural Japanese mountain conditions and keeps the foliage in top condition.

Lurking beneath the somewhat overgrown foliage of this *Cryptomeria* is a good branch structure. A year's pinching and pruning could return this little tree to its former glory.

Cryptomerias withstand sub-zero temperatures as long as they are protected from wind, and the roots are not waterlogged. However, under these conditions, the foliage may temporarily turn bronze or even deep reddish-brown. This looks somewhat worrying at first, but the fresh green color will soon return as the weather improves.

What to look for

Good health is indicated by bright green foliage. Any trees with yellow patches or accumulations of dead, dry foliage should be avoided. Search out an example with an obvious trunk line from the roots to the very top of the tree.

Points to watch

Cryptomerias are adapted to life on the sides of Japanese mountains, with their feet in moist but free-draining soil and their heads in the clouds. Imitate this and you will not go far wrong. The need to keep the inner branches clean and free from debris and unwanted shoots cannot be over emphasized.

CRYPTOMERIA JAPONICA

BONSAI SOURCES

Japan.

LIGHT LEVELS

Full sun to semi-shade.
In hot summers, protect from direct sun but ensure there is good overhead light.

TEMPERATURE RANGE

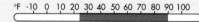

Minimum 25°C. Will withstand normal temperate or sub-tropical summers. Can be allowed to freeze for brief periods, but should be protected from prolonged or heavy frosts. Avoid cold winds at all costs.

PESTS AND DISEASES

Scale insects, mealy bug and spider mites are common. Mildew and gray mold occur when growing conditions are poor. All are easily treated.

SOIL

ORGANIC 60%	GRIT 40%

Repot every two to five years, depending on size of tree.

WATERING

SPRING	SUMMER	FALL	WINTER
🌢🌢	🌢🌢🌢	🌢🌢	🌢

Water well during growing season and keep moist in winter. Spray foliage regularly.

FEEDING

SPRING	SUMMER	FALL	WINTER
🌢	🌢	🌢	

Balanced feed throughout the growing season, topped up with nitrogen-free fertilizer in fall.

PRUNING

  Pinch out growing tips to maintain shape. Prune branches in late summer, while there is time for the healing process to begin before winter. Pruning in spring will encourage new shoots to grow in the area of the wound.

CYCAS

Cycad
TENDER

As the fronds become old and begin to wither they should be cut off close to the trunk with a sharp knife.

Cycas can survive with a very little root mass and infrequent repotting, which contributes to the reduction in size.

It is impossible to grow *Cycas* in any of the classical Japanese styles. Nevertheless, this bonsai is an almost exact replica of a full-sized tree, and creates the lush atmosphere of tropical islands.

CYCADS ARE COMMON in all tropical or subtropical regions, and are among the oldest of all species. They evolved from ferns and are the evolutionary link between ferns and trees. The two species used for bonsai cultivation, *Cycas revoluta* (sago palm) and *C. circinnalis*, both originate from China. In spite of the common name, cycads are only distantly related to true palms, although their growth pattern is similar.

Cycads grow from small bulb-like protrusions that form at the base of the trunk and easily break away and take root. As they grow, the trunks first become fat and round before gradually elongating to a more palm-like form.

The use of cycads as bonsai was developed in areas where our familiar tree-shapes are alien, and meaningless to the local bonsai enthusiasts. But even to Westerners, they have tremendous appeal, and are evocative of tropical paradise islands.

Cycads are extremely slow-growing, but nevertheless fascinating to cultivate. Wire training and branch pruning are clearly impossible. The only maintenance needed is the removal of dead fronds. These are best cut cleanly with a sharp knife, at a 45° angle close to the trunk. As this process is repeated over the years, the familiar "notched" palm-like trunk will develop. Careless removal of dead fronds will produce a ragged and untidy trunk. The restriction of the roots in a container is all that is needed to miniaturize the leaves and growth pattern.

Cycads grow naturally in areas

of high rainfall and humidity, so they love moisture and will not tolerate dry roots. This preference can be utilized for display purposes. If you want to exhibit your cycad, try gently easing it from the pot and standing the root ball in a dark-colored, shallow tray of water for a few days. You can apply a little moss to the sides of the root ball to insulate and disguise the roots. The image is of a tropical island, and the way the fronds reflect in the water fires the imagination.

What to look for

An example with several trunks of different sizes will ultimately make a more interesting bonsai. Check that the growing tip in the centre of the spiral of fronds is healthy. If no bud or emerging shoot can be seen, it may mean that drought has retarded growth. The plant will recover, but it is better not to buy one that needs nursing back to health.

Points to watch

Cycads are environmentally sensitive, and sudden changes in light, temperature, or exposure to drafts may cause all the fronds to die. But don't despair. Place the tree in a bright position, keep the pot warm and wet, and it will soon recover. The roots are thick, fleshy, and *very* fragile, so extreme care is needed when repotting.

CYCAS

BONSAI SOURCES

China.

LIGHT LEVELS

OUTSIDE   INSIDE

Full sun to semi-shade.
Avoid situations where the pot is in direct sun.

TEMPERATURE RANGE

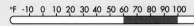

°F -10 0 10 20 30 40 50 60 70 80 90 100

As hot as you like. Minimum temperature 59°F. Best kept above 68°F at all times.

PESTS AND DISEASES

Virtually pest-free. Scale insects may attack from time to time. "Damping off" (a fungal infection familiar to gardeners that attacks the stems of young seedlings) may occur if the soil water is allowed to become stagnant or too cold.

SOIL

ORGANIC 80%	GRIT 20%

Repot every five years at most. Be extremely careful with the fragile roots. It may be better to leave the roots unpruned and repot into a fractionally larger container.

WATERING

SPRING	SUMMER	FALL	WINTER
💧💧💧	💧💧💧	💧💧💧	💧💧

Plenty of water all year round. In winter, reduce slightly to avoid becoming stagnant.

FEEDING

SPRING	SUMMER	FALL	WINTER
	💧 💧		

Half-strength balanced feed in summer, reduced to quarter-strength in the winter.

PRUNING

Cut off dead fronds as necessary.

FAGUS CRENATA

Japanese "white" beech

HARDY

BEECHES ARE LARGE, deciduous trees, common throughout the northern hemisphere. However, although all varieties can be trained into excellent bonsai, only the Japanese *Fagus crenata* is commercially produced. Here, again, the Japanese have got lucky – their beech has smaller, more dainty leaves with attractive "crimped" margins, finer twigs, and bark that becomes almost silvery white with age.

Japanese beech make fine single-trunk bonsai, but are at their best when planted in groups. The charm of a bonsai beech forest is further enhanced as the light green leaves turn yellow in fall, and then become a bright copper color and remain on the tree all winter, before finally falling just prior to the buds opening in spring. In nature, young beeches retain their dead leaves in winter to protect the buds from wind and snow, but older trees lose this tendency. In bonsai, however, the tendency persists, regardless of the age of the tree.

Branches set quickly when wire-trained, and pruning wounds heal rapidly. New buds regularly form on old wood after pruning. The one technique that should be avoided is leaf pruning. Although beech will quickly produce a second crop of leaves after defoliation, they are nothing like the original leaves.

This well-developed beech forest is just beginning to be a little untidy, and needs the first of its summer trimming sessions.

They are flatter, rounder and often twisted. In short, they are downright ugly! However, removing the odd oversized leaf to maintain the shape will not induce this odd foliage.

When you acquire your beech, it will probably have many thin branches which will need to be reduced in number so that the remaining ones can be positioned with wire and allowed to thicken. Pruning back all new shoots to one or two leaves as soon as they begin to darken in color will encourage more branching and finer twigs. If this routine is followed for a few years, a uniform tracery of twigs will develop which looks marvelous in winter – if you can bear to remove the dead, copper-colored leaves.

What to look for

Beech are generally propagated from cuttings, and there is a chance that some smaller bonsai have been potted up before their root systems have properly developed. Check the roots are holding the tree firmly in its pot.

When buying a group or forest planting, examine the composition. The trunks should vary in size, with the thickest and tallest towards the front and off-center. The thickness and height of the other trunks should decrease towards the back and sides to create the illusion of perspective. If you keep this in mind when you look at a number of examples, you will be amazed at how much this simple rule contributes to the realism of the composition.

Points to watch

Japanese white beech are easy to grow and maintain, but the foliage is easily scorched at the edges by warm or cold winds, or if the soil is allowed to become too dry in hot weather. The answer is not to water more heavily, but to shelter the tree from wind at all times. Allowing water droplets to remain on the leaves in hot sun will also cause localized scorching as they act as tiny magnifying glasses.

The many trunks of different thicknesses are arranged to create the illusion of depth and perspective. The shallow container enhances this effect.

FAGUS CRENATA

BONSAI SOURCES

Japan.

LIGHT LEVELS

 OUTSIDE   INSIDE

Full sun to semi-shade.
Can be brought indoors for display for brief periods during summer, but never in winter.

TEMPERATURE RANGE

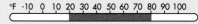
°F -10 0 10 20 30 40 50 60 70 80 90 100

Unsuitable for hot climates where summer temperatures regularly remain above 86°F. Tolerates freezing well, but should be placed in a shed or garage during prolonged spells of less than 15°F.

PESTS AND DISEASES

 Aphids are a nuisance as they distort shoots and produce sticky "honeydew" which discolors foliage and harbors fungal spores. Scale insects and leaf-eating insects are also troublesome. Powdery mildew occurs in poor ventilation.

SOIL

ORGANIC 60%	GRIT 40%

Repot every two to three years, either in late winter or in fall if some protection can be given against freezing for more than a day or so.

WATERING

SPRING	SUMMER	FALL	WINTER
●●●	●●●	●●	●●

Water daily in summer and keep moist at all times in winter. Do not allow the soil to become dry at any time.

FEEDING

SPRING	SUMMER	FALL	WINTER
●	●	●	

Balanced feed from late spring to midsummer. Nitrogen-free feed from late summer until leaves turn yellow. Do not feed until four weeks after leaves have emerged.

PRUNING

 Trim shoots to one or two leaves to maintain shape. Prune branches in late winter or early spring. Prune close to the trunk, leaving no stubs.

FICUS

Fig varieties

TENDER

THE VARIETIES OF fig used for bonsai are more closely related to the familiar "rubber plant" than the large tree with edible fruits, whose leaves were used to preserve the modesty of Adam and Eve. *Ficus retusa* and *F. benjamina* are jungle plants native to Southeast Asia and, as such, require warmth, humidity, and some shade. *F. microphylla* originates from Australia, and can tolerate a little more sun, although it will grow well in semi-shade.

Bonsai figs are typified by their leathery, pointed oval leaves and slender twigs. They also naturally produce aerial roots – heavy, tough roots which grow in large numbers from the upper trunk and branches. In nature, these roots stabilize the tree in stormy climates and swampy soil. Eventually, they take over the function of the original trunk, forming a dense grove. Rather than trying to prevent these aerial roots, the bonsai artists of Southeast Asia incorporate them into the design, creating images that are so evocative of the steamy rainforests.

Very much like willow, all figs root readily from cuttings taken from thick, old branches, so a very mature-looking bonsai can be created in a relatively short time. Often, these thick-rooted cuttings are planted with the roots wrapped around rocks. The roots quickly thicken and appear to clasp the rocks tightly, forming the "root-over-rock" style. On commercial bonsai, little attention is paid to the arrangement of the roots and, as often as not, there are far too many of them in a tangled mass. These should be thinned out over two or three years, cutting away thinner or crossing roots and leaving the thicker ones until a more natural arrangement is achieved.

Even tiny trees like this can have well-tapered trunks and a good basic branch structure. Leaf pruning in midsummer could induce summer foliage.

FAR LEFT
Constant trimming and annual leaf pruning will gradually reduce the leaf size on this moderately priced fig. A new cloud of foliage can be developed, which will conceal the exaggerated curve halfway up the trunk.

LEFT
This slanting-style *Ficus* is typical of the many medium-priced trees arriving in the West each year. The trunk and basic branch structure provide a good basis for further development.

When figs are wounded, they produce a milky latex which is the plants' defence mechanism against infection. This latex can be produced in enormous quantities, especially when the plant is in full growth. When dry, it is difficult to remove from the branches.

Defoliating in midsummer encourages a new crop of small leaves and fine twigs.

What to look for
Choose a plant that already has a good branch structure, as new branches are slow to grow in domestic environments. Check the base of the trunk to ensure that the base of the original cutting is below soil level.

Points to watch
Prune only in winter and seal all wounds immediately, either with modeling clay or by *briefly* applying a red-hot screwdriver or similar, to cauterize the wound. Check wire regularly – it will mark the bark rapidly. Figs dislike drafts and sudden changes in temperature or humidity.

FICUS

BONSAI SOURCES

Throughout Southeast Asia.

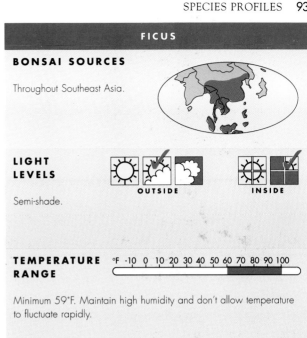

LIGHT LEVELS

OUTSIDE   INSIDE

Semi-shade.

TEMPERATURE RANGE

°F -10 0 10 20 30 40 50 60 70 80 90 100

Minimum 59°F. Maintain high humidity and don't allow temperature to fluctuate rapidly.

PESTS AND DISEASES

Scale insects.

SOIL

ORGANIC 60%	GRIT 40%

Repot every two years in late winter. Can be repotted with care at most other times. Keeping pot warm after repotting aids rapid growth of new roots.

WATERING

SPRING	SUMMER	FALL	WINTER

Water well in summer and keep soil well moistened in winter.

FEEDING

SPRING	SUMMER	FALL	WINTER

Balanced feed while in growth, reduce to half strength during winter.

PRUNING

Prune in winter and seal cuts immediately to prevent "bleeding".

FUCHSIA

Fuchsia
TENDER

ORIGINALLY FROM CENTRAL and South America and New Zealand, fuchsias are now grown for their flowers all over the world as garden and greenhouse plants. Each year, new varieties are introduced with ever more spectacular color variations and larger blooms. However, these modern varieties are of little use for bonsai because their leaves are generally too large and their flowers far too showy.

The varieties used for bonsai are the small-leaved ones such as *Fuchsia microphylla* with equally small, but nevertheless charming flowers borne in summer. The papery bark ranges from buff to orange-red, and it can adopt an aged appearance even in young plants when growth is restricted.

Fuchsias produce flowers on the current year's growth, so their annual pruning should be carried out in late winter or early spring. Cut back much further than you would if just pruning to shape. The tree may look a little bare for a while, but you need to leave room for flower-bearing shoots to elongate without outgrowing the final shape of the tree. When each shoot has six or seven pairs of leaves, they can be cut back to four or five pairs. Once a shoot has finished flowering, it can be cut back again, leaving just one pair of leaves. New shoots will grow from the base of these leaves and, with luck, the flowering cycle will be repeated. Don't carry out this second pruning from late summer onward, as there won't be time for a second flush of flowers before fall, and the resulting new shoots may be too weak to survive the winter.

Although many fuchsias are frost hardy when grown in the ground, they die down to ground level in cold winters. When grown in containers, the roots also die when frozen, so fuchsia bonsai should be regarded as tender. Having said this, it is essential for their health and for good flowering that they are given a resting period where temperatures remain between 40–50°F for three months. During dormancy, they may lose some or all of their leaves, depending on growing conditions. Keep in mind that a plant with leaves will require more water at this time than one without leaves.

All fuchsias appreciate being sprayed with fresh water, daily in summer, and less frequently during the winter.

The tiny compact leaves and small pendulous flowers are in perfect proportion to the size and shape of this wonderful specimen fuchsia. The sensitively placed rocks add a sense of scale and realism.

Although young, this little fuchsia shows promise with pleasing trunk line and well-spaced branches.

What to look for

Many fuchsia bonsai are homegrown and may not have the same interesting trunk characteristics as imported trees, so take time to seek out the best of the batch. Ensure that the leaves and flowers are small. Fuchsias do have a tendency to allow branches to die back if growing conditions are poor – and nursery shelves are far from ideal. Don't buy a bonsai with dead branches; this may be a sign of serious problems with the roots.

Points to watch

Although fuchsias can be wire-trained at any time, their branches are very brittle and snap easily. It is best to wire in winter and to allow the soil to become a little dry for a day or so beforehand. This reduces the water present in the plant's cells and makes the branches a little more flexible.

FUCHSIA

BONSAI SOURCES

Most bonsai are produced in the Far East. Some are home-produced as well.

LIGHT LEVELS

Full sun.
Ensure pots are shaded when kept outdoors in summer.

TEMPERATURE RANGE

°F -10 0 10 20 30 40 50 60 70 80 90 100
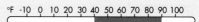

During winter maintain between 40°F and 50°F. Can be kept indoors or outside in summer. Keep humid at all times indoors.

PESTS AND DISEASES

Aphids and scale insects occur in all situations. Red spider mite can appear on plants growing indoors. Minor attacks are made by black spot fungi.

SOIL

ORGANIC 60%	GRIT 40%

Repot every year.

WATERING

SPRING	SUMMER	FALL	WINTER

Water frequently when in growth. Reduce watering when dormant.

FEEDING

SPRING	SUMMER	FALL	WINTER

Balanced feed in spring, low nitrogen in summer and a final nitrogen-free feed in early fall.

PRUNING

Branch pruning in late winter or early spring; cut all shoots back hard. Trim shoots to four or five pairs of leaves in summer and cut to shape after flowering.

GINKGO BILOBA

Maidenhair tree

HARDY

THIS IS THE oldest living species on earth, and thought to be extinct until it was rediscovered in China in the seventeenth century. It is a primitive type of conifer with fan-shaped leaves similar to those of the maidenhair fern, and is now commonly planted in streets and gardens all over the world.

Ginkgo bonsai are produced in Japan to a unique style which imitates the columnar shape of an old, mature tree in the wild. However, this is not entirely by design. Ginkgo resents pruning, and pruned shoots are inclined to die back further, either shortly after pruning or, more annoyingly, during winter. This results in a heavy, tapered trunk with a few short, upward-facing branches. Twigs grow in clusters from the branches and, as the cycle of growth and replacement is repeated, it results in large, gnarled areas. Not all shoots will die back, though, and those that survive are used to build branches.

Needless to say, producing a ginkgo bonsai is a slow process, and prices of specimen trees reflect this. However, fairly substantial plants are exported from Japan at a reasonable price. These are field-grown trunks which have been lifted and planted in deeper-than-usual containers for a year or two. They are by no means fully-developed bonsai, but can

It takes many years to develop a strong, gnarled trunk on ginkgoes. This semi-specimen is almost there – just a few more years will be needed to complete the image.

provide you with a good basic trunk to work from.

The unique ginkgo style does not require wire training – which is fortunate because the bark can be easily damaged.

When pruning ginkgo, remember that the wounds do not heal over as they do with almost every other species. These unhealed wounds can be ugly when pruning is carelessly done. Try not to damage the bark around the wound – leave short stubs and remove them carefully a year later, when they have dried out.

Don't be too con-cerned if your ginkgo doesn't grow too much some years. They have a habit of putting on very little growth one year and bolting the next.

GINKGO BILOBA

BONSAI SOURCES

Japan.

LIGHT LEVELS

OUTSIDE   **INSIDE**

Full sun or semi-shade.

TEMPERATURE RANGE

°F -10 0 10 20 30 40 50 60 70 80 90 100

Tolerates light freezing for brief periods. Best kept in an insulated garage or shed during coldest months. Do not keep in a heated room in winter.

PESTS AND DISEASES

Virtually pest-free.

SOIL

ORGANIC **70%**	GRIT **30%**

Repot every year in late winter/early spring and keep frost-free until new growth starts.

WATERING

SPRING	SUMMER	FALL	WINTER

Water generously in summer; keep soil barely moist in winter. Spray foliage regularly.

FEEDING

SPRING	SUMMER	FALL	WINTER

Balanced feed in summer, nitrogen-free from early fall.

PRUNING

Prune new shoots to shape as necessary. Prune to a leaf facing in the direction of desired new growth. Remove all dead material in early spring, when swelling buds will indicate live shoots.

RIGHT
Younger ginkgoes are often grown as clumps. Heavy pruning carried out at regular intervals can develop an unusual and interesting bonsai from this type of stock.

What to look for

Since most of the existing twigs will either die back or will be replaced, it is important to select a starter tree with an interesting trunk, good root spread, and at least some established, short branches. Areas of dieback are normal and are not necessarily a sign of ill-health.

Points to watch

Ginkgo have thick, fleshy roots which hold a lot of moisture. When they become frozen the water expands and the roots can literally explode with the pressure, particularly when there is an imbalance in the water content of the roots and the soil. It is far easier to keep the tree free from prolonged or severe freezing than it is to maintain constant moisture level in the soil.

ILEX CRENATA

Japanese holly

HARDY

UNLIKE THE EUROPEAN holly, with its dark green leaves with needle-sharp points along the margins, this variety has very small, oval leaves with no sharp points. Ironically, just to confuse the matter, one of the Japanese common names for this variety is English holly! It is frequently used in the West as well as the East as a hedging plant because of the obliging way it responds to clipping by producing masses of fine, dense twigs.

The trunks and branches tend to appear pretty fleshy because of the unusually thick bark, but the shoots that emerge are thin and, although

brittle, can be wire-trained and manipulated into shape. However, the slow growth rate means that the branches may take a year or two to set in position. You will need to check the wire regularly because the bark swells rapidly and can easily become scarred, especially at the top of the tree. As soon as the wire

appears to be about to cut into the bark, remove it immediately and, if necessary, reapply it. This time, coil the wire in the opposite direction to avoid the risk of it creating a double spiral of marks, and to allow the sap-conducting tissues under the first wire room to grow and expand.

Japanese holly blooms readily, but the flowers are small, pale greenish-white, and difficult to spot. Male and female flowers are borne on separate plants, so the small, berries will only set on female plants, and then only if fertilized by a nearby male. The other characteristics of the plant – its bark, twigs, and foliage – make it a first-class subject for bonsai.

Japanese holly is one of the few species that can be grown equally as well indoors as outside, since it is equally content in full sun or shade, and it does not require particularly cold winters to provide a dormant period. When growing the plant indoors, spray the foliage with fresh water daily in summer, to imitate the conditions in the tree's natural, woodland floor habitat.

When grown outside, Japanese holly needs protection from anything more than a mild frost. The twigs and foliage can cope with heavy frosts, but the thick, fleshy roots will burst as the water in them expands as it freezes. An unheated

Japanese holly is grown primarily for its fruit, but you will need plants of both sexes to achieve success. However, even without fruit, the attractive trunk lines and foliage of this specimen clump-style bonsai make it a worthwhile tree to buy.

These small, inexpensive "starter" trees have all the potential to make fine bonsai in time. Given the choice, the cascade bonsai on the right would be the best buy because of its more developed trunk and gracefully cascading lower left-hand branch.

greenhouse or a windowsill in an unheated room will make ideal winter quarters.

What to look for

Heavy branches are impossible to reshape, so they should be evenly distributed and not so thick that they are disproportionate to the trunk. The thick roots can form very interesting and attractive surface formations, so it is worth keeping this feature in mind. Ugly pruning scars or wire marks can take a long time to heal, so beware of these.

Points to watch

If you can't find a suitable room or shed to overwinter your holly, place it on a low platform of bricks in a sheltered corner of the yard. Insulate the pot with several layers of styrofoam or glass-fiber fleece.

As the healing tissue covers pruning wounds, it also forms a swelling. Hollow out large wounds so the new tissue can grow into the recess, making less of a swelling.

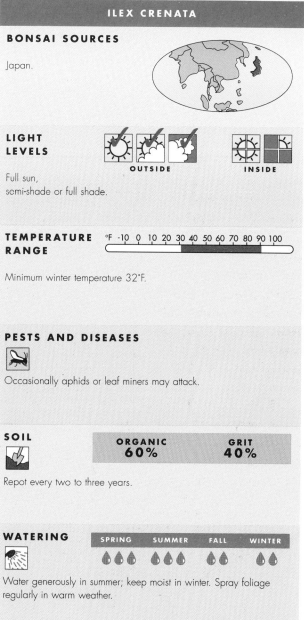

ILEX CRENATA

BONSAI SOURCES

Japan.

LIGHT LEVELS

OUTSIDE   INSIDE

Full sun, semi-shade or full shade.

TEMPERATURE RANGE

°F -10 0 10 20 30 40 50 60 70 80 90 100

Minimum winter temperature 32°F.

PESTS AND DISEASES

Occasionally aphids or leaf miners may attack.

SOIL

ORGANIC	GRIT
60%	40%

Repot every two to three years.

WATERING

SPRING	SUMMER	FALL	WINTER
🌢🌢🌢	🌢🌢🌢	🌢🌢	🌢🌢

Water generously in summer; keep moist in winter. Spray foliage regularly in warm weather.

FEEDING

SPRING	SUMMER	FALL	WINTER
🌢	🌢	🌢	

Balanced fertilizer in the growing season. Nitrogen-free feed in fall.

PRUNING

Trim to shape as necessary. Prune branches in fall or in early spring, before new growth starts.

JASMINUM NUDIFLORUM

Winter jasmine

HARDY

THIS NATIVE OF China has become one of the most popular winter-flowering shrubs throughout the West. Whether planted in full sun or in the dullest, coldest corner of the yard, its rich yellow flowers, borne on dark green, leafless stems will brighten the darkest of mid-winter days. When grown in a bonsai pot and shaped like a tree, its charm is magnified as it provides color when everything else is dormant, and in the northern hemisphere, it can make a stunning centerpiece for the Christmas dinner table.

The toughness of this seemingly delicate little plant is ideal for bonsai cultivation. It positively enjoys hard pruning and it can withstand frozen roots for a week or more at a time. The exception is when it is in flower. At this time, the roots must be free to absorb moisture for at least part of the day, so in order to avoid repetitive freezing and thawing, it is best to keep the tree at just above freezing while in bloom. When the flowering period is over it can be returned to the mercy of the weather. Jasmine flowers on last year's shoots, producing a single bloom from almost every leaf axil (the point where last year's leaves joined the shoot). To encourage flowering, prune new shoots to one pair of

leaves in midsummer. Allow the second flush of shoots to grow unchecked until late summer, then, as the growth slows down, prune again to about four pairs of leaves. You can vary the length of the shoots according to the shape of the tree, but pruning too hard will encourage a third, non-flowering set of weak shoots. Old flowering shoots will need to be pruned back to a pair of young shoots from time to time, in order to keep the twigs open and in proportion to the trunk.

Pruning for flower production makes wiring impractical. But the angular growth pattern and the prolific back budding make it also unnecessary. Any shape or style can be achieved simply by pruning away unwanted branches and allowing shoots for new branches to grow unchecked for a season, until they

Twin-trunk jasmines are unusual, and this one is a beauty. It would be a desirable bonsai in its own right even without the flowers.

Jasmines are slow to grow, so most commercial bonsai need much further development. This one provides a useful, sturdy trunk and plenty of potential branches with which to work.

thicken. Pruning back hard in winter will encourage many new, vigorous shoots the following year. Selected ones can be treated in the same way, while the rest are removed. In this way you can quickly build a simple branch structure on which the cycle of pruning for flowers can be performed.

What to look for
Jasmine grows slowly, so most commercial bonsai are small. It is difficult to develop an aged appearance on a commercial scale, so you should look for a sturdy-looking trunk and evenly arranged surface roots. Choose a tree whose main branches are already well distributed – the rest will be replaced by you in a year or so.

Points to watch
No bonsai likes exposure to cold winter winds, and jasmine, too, should receive some shelter from the worst of these. Although the roots are tough, they do not appreciate being waterlogged for long periods, especially when the pot is repeatedly frozen at night and partially thawed during the day.

JASMINUM NUDIFLORUM

BONSAI SOURCES
China. Because of its popularity as a small bonsai, many Western nurseries are now producing jasmine bonsai commercially.

LIGHT LEVELS

OUTSIDE **INSIDE**

From full sun to shade. Small pots should be shaded from full sun.

TEMPERATURE RANGE
°F -10 0 10 20 30 40 50 60 70 80 90 100

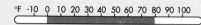

Minimum 15°F (32°F when in flower). Does not like prolonged exposure to hot sun when temperatures are constantly above 86°F.

PESTS AND DISEASES

Aphids and mealy-bug may attack young shoots.

SOIL

ORGANIC 60%	GRIT 40%

Repot every one to two years as soon as the last flowers have fallen. Can be repotted in fall, but this may retard flowering for the following winter.

WATERING

SPRING	SUMMER	FALL	WINTER
🌢🌢🌢	🌢🌢🌢	🌢🌢	🌢🌢

Water well in summer; keep evenly moist in winter.

FEEDING

SPRING	SUMMER	FALL	WINTER
🌢	🌢	🌢	

Balanced feed in spring, low-nitrogen feed in summer. One dose of nitrogen-free feed in fall.

PRUNING

Prune first flush of new shoots hard. Prune second flush to shape at the end of the summer. Thin out old flowering shoots in spring.

JUNIPERUS CHINENSIS SARGENTII

Sargent's juniper

HARDY

THE JAPANESE VARIETY of Chinese juniper – *shimpaku* – is not only arguably the easiest of all species to work on, but collected wild specimens certainly make the most dramatic and impressive bonsai.

In its natural habitat in the mountains of Japan, this small, spreading tree forms twisted, gnarled trunks and branches. It has a natural defence mechanism which restricts the foliage mass to ease the load on the roots in inhospitable conditions. It allows certain branches, or entire areas of the tree, to die off. The bark connecting these areas with the roots also dies and falls away, revealing the twisted grain of the wood. In time, this "driftwood" becomes bleached by the sun and contrasts vividly with the chestnut-brown bark and rich green foliage.

This natural characteristic is integrated into the design of specimen shimpaku bonsai, and additional areas of driftwood are often artificially introduced. In smaller bonsai, the areas of driftwood are all artificially created, but are no less valid or attractive.

Chinese junipers are tough and resilient, with very flexible branches. Pruning and wiring can be done at any time of year. Even repotting can be carried out at any time except during the two hottest months. New shoots are trimmed as necessary by grasping tufts of foliage between the thumb and forefinger of one hand and simply pulling off the tips with the other. In this way, a clearly defined foliage cloud can be maintained. All foliage growing down from the undersides of the branches should be cut away completely to keep the branch lines neat.

Towards the end of the growing season, the extending shoots – distinguished by their lighter color and fatter appearance – should be cut back to the first small side shoots. This allows light and air to

This semi-specimen shimpaku was grown with a final design in mind (unlike the smaller tree opposite). The curves in the trunk were introduced when the tree was still young, and the carefully selected branches have been trained to cascade from the trunk with wire. Routine pinching and trimming will further enhance the image as the years pass.

This simple juniper is really little more than a rooted cutting that has been allowed to grow unchecked for a couple of years. Although it looks like a little tree at the moment, it does not have the potential to become a fine bonsai. A longer trunk with branches wired downward would be a better buy.

penetrate the inner areas and generates new growth from branch intersections.

If you want to create a new driftwood branch (*jin*) or area of the trunk (*shari*), do this in late summer, when there is still time for the wound to heal. Once the wood is dry, it can be bleached and preserved with lime-sulphur solution. Ensure that all the living branches remain directly connected to the roots by a line of living bark.

What to look for
Commercial shimpakus have artificially-shaped trunks and some will be better than others. Choose a trunk that appeals to you. The branches and foliage can be rearranged later if you are not entirely happy with it.

Points to watch
Sometimes branches will die for no apparent reason. It's not your fault – this is something the species does naturally from time to time. If you don't regularly cut out the extending shoots, the inner foliage will die off, spoiling the compact shape.

JUNIPERUS CHINENSIS SARGENTII

BONSAI SOURCES
Japan.

LIGHT LEVELS

Full sun to light shade.
Growth is more compact when in full sun, but color improves in semi-shade.

TEMPERATURE RANGE
°F -10 0 10 20 30 40 50 60 70 80 90 100
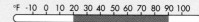
Minimum 15°F. Prolonged freezing causes foliage to turn bronze, but it will regain its rich green color in spring. Do not keep indoors.

PESTS AND DISEASES

Tiny scale insects can colonize the plant unnoticed. The telltale signs are yellowing foliage and minute white specks on the shoots. Water systemic insecticide into the soil. Fungal infections are rare.

SOIL

| ORGANIC 40% | GRIT 60% |
Adding some finely chopped, fresh sphagnum moss (the kind used to line hanging flower baskets) to the soil seems to benefit the plant.

WATERING

| SPRING | SUMMER | FALL | WINTER |
Water well in summer and keep moist in winter. Although drought tolerant, junipers are also thirsty – surprisingly so in winter.

FEEDING

| SPRING | SUMMER | FALL | WINTER |
Half-strength balanced feed all growing season.

PRUNING

Any time. Wounds may "bleed" in hottest months of summer.

JUNIPERUS RIGIDA

Needle juniper

HARDY

THE ALTERNATIVE COMMON name for this variety, 'temple juniper,' indicates the special spiritual significance it has in its native Japan. Unlike its cousins, *J. rigida* has very sharp needle-like leaves, carried in groups of three on slender shoots. On a mature tree in the wild, these shoots hang loosely from the arching branches and sway freely in the wind.

Because the young shoots are so slender, they can sometimes give a bonsai an unkempt appearance if allowed to grow too long, so regular trimming is necessary. At the base of each needle is a dormant bud which will invariably produce a new shoot after trimming. The more severe the trimming, the greater the number of these dormant buds that will extend. This combination inevitably results in overcrowded foliage masses which are a paradise for red spider mites and fungal spores. To prevent this occurring, prune away the outer ends of the older twigs once a year, leaving the young shoots growing from further back towards the main branches. These young shoots will grow on to replace the pruned twigs and, in time, the process is repeated.

The importance of this twig pruning cycle cannot be over-emphasized. Allowing light and air to penetrate the inner branches not only helps keep pests at

bay, but also stimulates the growth of new shoots and keeps the whole branch healthy. As well as harboring pests, over-crowded foliage causes dieback of many twigs and weakens the entire branch.

In common with Chinese juniper, needle junipers naturally form large natural areas of driftwood when grown in the mountains. These already gnarled and twisted areas are further sculpted by wind and rain and can become really bizarre. You can create your own driftwood by following the process outlined on page 103.

Most specimen needle junipers have large areas of natural "driftwood" – called *shari*. These are bleached and preserved with lime sulphur.

The young branches are very supple, although less so than Chinese juniper, but become more brittle with age. If you want to change the position of a branch by wiring, test it gently first. If it seems a little stiff, stagger the repositioning over a period of several months, moving it bit by bit each week.

Small commercial needle junipers seldom have *sharis*. Instead, they are frequently wired to the twisted trunk.

Needle junipers develop tight foliage which can harbor pests if allowed to become too congested. When the foliage reaches this stage, it should be thinned to allow light and air to penetrate.

The flaky outer bark can be gently brushed away, revealing the orange-red under-bark which contrasts beautifully with the silver-gray driftwood and subtle color of the foliage.

What to look for

First, check that the roots are holding the tree firm in its pot. Any weak-rooted plants should be avoided as root problems are difficult to rectify in this species. Select a tree with a sturdy, interesting trunk with exciting and natural-looking driftwood. Trees with overcrowded foliage should be left on the shelf.

Points to watch

Watch the soil quality and watering carefully. Problems with the roots can take over twelve months to visually affect the foliage. By the time you discover the problem, the tree may be beyond recovery. Areas of discolored foliage that cannot be attributed to spider mites or scale insects must be pruned back to healthy growth and burned. Rare and difficult to diagnose fungi can invade needle junipers and may kill the tree if allowed to spread.

BONSAI SOURCES

Japan.

LIGHT LEVELS

OUTSIDE   **INSIDE**

Full sun.
Do not keep indoors.

TEMPERATURE RANGE

°F -10 0 10 20 30 40 50 60 70 80 90 100

Minimum 15°F. Foliage may turn bronze in very cold spells, but recovers its green color in spring. Protect from cold winds.

PESTS AND DISEASES

Scale insects, spider mites and small caterpillars are easily eradicated. Rare fungal attacks can be controlled by pruning out affected branches.

SOIL

ORGANIC 40%	GRIT 60%

The addition of some fresh, chopped sphagnum moss (the kind used to line hanging flower baskets) can help keep the soil conditions favorable.

WATERING

SPRING	SUMMER	FALL	WINTER
🌢🌢	🌢🌢🌢	🌢🌢	🌢

Water well in summer, but avoid waterlogging. Keep moist but not wet during winter.

FEEDING

SPRING	SUMMER	FALL	WINTER
🌢	🌢	🌢	

Balanced feed at half strength all growing season. Top up with two applications of nitrogen-free fertilizer in early fall.

PRUNING

Prune branches at any time provided frost is not expected. Cut or pinch out growing tips as necessary to maintain shape. Thin out old growth regularly to prevent overcrowding of the foliage.

JUNIPERUS SQUAMATA 'MEYERI'

Meyer's juniper

HARDY

ORIGINALLY FROM NEPAL, this species has parented a number of varieties which have become immensely popular as garden plants throughout the world. One such variety, *J. s.* 'Meyeri', has also become one of the most common subjects for home-produced bonsai in the West. It has all the favorable attributes of Chinese juniper – hardiness, flexible branches, compact growth and attractive bark – but has beautiful, feathery, silver-blue foliage.

Although rarely imported from the East, Meyer's juniper bonsai are so frequently produced by Western nurseries that it has been included in this book.

The slender, rather floppy young shoots are densely clothed with soft blue needles which point forwards, almost hugging the shoot. As the shoot extends, the needles stand more erect and expose the tiny dormant buds nestling at the base. The natural growth pattern is extremely dense, so once the basic branch structure has been established – which should already have been done by the nursery – the major work is confined to constantly thinning out the older shoots in order to give the newer ones room to develop.

Any new shoots that break the upper outline of the foliage clouds

The rough, outer bark has been carefully cleaned away with a wire brush to reveal the wonderful smooth, orange-red inner layer, which contrasts with the subtle shapes and tones of the driftwood areas.

can be pinched back with the finger tips. Don't worry if you occasionally pull away an entire shoot. It will quickly be replaced by a new one. The rather floppy nature of the shoots means that many of them

will grow downward from the undersides of the branches. These must be removed entirely, either by pulling them out or, if they are older, cutting them off at their point of origin.

Hardly a bonsai, this squamata is in the very early stages of training. With careful carving of the sawn-off branches and positioning of the new shoots, it has the potential to become a superb specimen one day.

Like most junipers, Meyer's juniper will issue adventitious shoots from branch intersections and from where branches meet the trunk. These should also be removed as soon as they appear unless you want to use them to regenerate branches or to build up new foliage clouds.

What to look for
Homeproduced bonsai may lack the finesse of imported trees, so you would be wise to choose one that is clearly underdeveloped, and thereby allow yourself the opportunity to finish the job. Look for a trunk that has a series of curves, rather than sharp angles which look unnatural.

Points to watch
Congested foliage encourages spider mites which seem to prefer this species to all others. However, they are easily treated with systemic insecticide. The young shoots are precariously fixed to the branches and are easily knocked off when wiring or with careless pruning. They will regenerate in time, but it is best to try to avoid dislodging them in the first place.

This specimen squamata was developed from a garden shrub, a practice which is common among serious bonsai enthusiasts. Yards are good sources for bonsai material.

JUNIPERUS SQUAMATA 'MEYERI'

BONSAI SOURCES

Bonsai produced throughout the West.

LIGHT LEVELS

OUTSIDE · INSIDE

Full sun.
Will tolerate semi-shade, but growth becomes less sturdy.

TEMPERATURE RANGE °F -10 0 10 20 30 40 50 60 70 80 90 100

Minimum 15°F. Cold winds will damage young shoots, so keep sheltered. May be brought indoors for a day or so at a time during the winter.

PESTS AND DISEASES

Spider mites are the main enemy. Scale insects and small web-weaving caterpillars can be a problem. Fungal infections can attack congested foliage. Treat with systemic fungicide.

SOIL | ORGANIC 40% | GRIT 60%

Repot every two years in spring.

WATERING | SPRING | SUMMER | FALL | WINTER

Water well in summer; keep moist but not wet in winter. Spray foliage regularly with cold water all year.

FEEDING | SPRING | SUMMER | FALL | WINTER

Balanced feed all growing season. Top up with nitrogen-free feed in the fall.

PRUNING

Prune branches at any time. Foliage must be regularly trimmed and thinned out to ensure healthy growth. Remove all the downward-growing shoots.

LAGERSTROEMIA INDICA

Crape myrtle

TENDER

FOR GENERATIONS THIS attractive, deciduous, subtropical shrub has been popular as a garden plant in the Mediterranean region, South America and the southern United States. Originally from China and Korea, crape myrtle is grown for its short-lived but showy display of flowers which can range in color from deep lilac, through pinks to almost white.

For the bonsai collector, crape myrtle has more to offer than just its flowers. It sheds outer layers of bark from time to time and, depending on the season, the color of the underlying bark can vary from pale gray through rusty-brown to almost pink. The result is an extremely attractive patchwork of subtle colors which is particularly spectacular in fall and winter when there are no leaves to obscure the bark.

The fact that this species is deciduous means that it is necessary to keep it pretty cool – but frost-free – during winter in order to guarantee a sufficient dormant period. Without this, the tree would become exhausted and would eventually die. Reducing the light level and maintaining the soil barely moist during winter also helps the plant to rest.

Crape myrtles flower on short shoots of the current year's growth, so to encourage prolific blossoming

Delicate mid-green leaves are borne on fine twigs which can become quite dense with regular pinching of new growth.

you need to be fairly careful how and when you prune. Heavy branches can be pruned in fall, and the wounds should be well sealed. In spring, allow the new shoots to grow untouched for several weeks, until the leaves begin to harden and the rate of extension slows down. This should take you up to late spring or early summer, at which time you can cut all these new shoots back to two or three leaves. The buds at the axils of these leaves will produce a fresh crop of lateral, flower-bearing shoots. Flowering can be further encouraged by reducing the nitrogen content of the fertilizer. Brand tomato or rose feeds are ideal for this purpose.

What to look for

Search for an example with a thick attractive trunk line – the thicker the trunk, the more bark to appreciate! If buying in late fall or winter, avoid any trees that are still in leaf. They will not perform well for you.

Points to watch

Crape myrtles *must* have a sufficient dormant period. Maintain winter temperatures between 45–50°F, and allow light levels to fall while bare of leaves. Reinstate good light as soon as buds start to swell in spring. Do not prune away lateral growth in midsummer unless you are prepared to miss out on the flowering period for a year.

Removing some of the upper branches and shortening the others would help strengthen the two weak lower branches.

The trunk, although still slender, is beginning to show the characteristic flaking which creates an ever-changing pattern on mature trees.

LAGERSTROEMIA INDICA

BONSAI SOURCES

Bonsai exported from China and Korea and also home-produced in some western subtropical regions.

LIGHT LEVELS

 OUTSIDE

 INSIDE

Bright and airy situation in summer. Can be grown outdoors in summer in temperate zones after acclimatization. Reduce light levels in fall to induce dormancy.

TEMPERATURE RANGE

°F -10 0 10 20 30 40 50 60 70 80 90 100

Untroubled by high temperatures during summer provided light and humidity are also high. Maintain at between 45–50°F during winter. Never expose to frost.

PESTS AND DISEASES

Generally pest-free, although aphids and mildew can be a problem on neglected plants.

SOIL

ORGANIC 60%	GRIT 40%

Repot every one to three years, depending on size.

WATERING

SPRING	SUMMER	FALL	WINTER

Water well during growing season, without allowing soil to become waterlogged. In winter, maintain soil just moist, increasing water as the buds begin to swell in spring. Too much water during flowering will make blossoms fall prematurely.

FEEDING

SPRING	SUMMER	FALL	WINTER

Low-nitrogen feed throughout the growing season. Nitrogen-free feed in the fall.

PRUNING

Prune heavy branches in fall. To encourage flowering, cut spring growth back to three to four internodes in late spring. Trim to shape in fall.

LIGUSTRUM SINENSE

Chinese privet

HARDY

Although slender-trunked, this privet has a reasonable branch structure which could form the basis of a fine bonsai. The vigorous shoots at the top indicate the tree's good health.

will reward the owner with a mass of sweetly fragrant tiny white blossoms borne on small, upright spikes which contrast with the rich leaves.

Unlike leaves, which can be encouraged to reduce in size, flowers on a bonsai will always be full-sized. However, if a plant produces flower heads comprising hundreds of individual blooms, the flower heads themselves can be trimmed to shape and size by cutting cleanly through the flower stalks. This not only maintains an appropriate sense of scale, but it also reduces the strain on the reduced root system and reduces the risk of the plant expending too much energy of flower production.

Ligustrum bonsai are produced in China, Taiwan and Korea, and can follow almost any style. Prolific back budding means that the trunks and main branches can rapidly become obscured beneath a mass of twigs and foliage. This is one of the "busy" species – there will always be something that needs doing. Pinching out the rapidly growing shoots, rubbing off unwanted buds, training in new branches, etc.

The young roots are very thick and fleshy, but they soon become woody. This helps the bonsai grower by aiding the formation of attractive surface roots. However, it has the disadvantage of filling the pot with

ALTHOUGH A HARDY shrub, this species is nevertheless capable of thriving in subtropical conditions or of being kept indoors all year round in temperate zones. It is semi-deciduous – meaning that in warmer regions the leaves remain on the plant all year round, but in colder parts of the world some or all of the leaves are shed in fall.

The common privet used throughout the world as a hedging plant has a reputation for being dry and dusty, for draining the nearby soil of nutrients, and for being generally unpleasant. This unfair reputation has caused many bonsai retailers to rename Chinese privet as "wood holly," "mountain laurel" and many other misleading names in order to increase its appeal to the public. This should not be necessary, as privet is an excellent plant for bonsai training. It responds well to pruning, root pruning, wiring and trimming and, if allowed to flower,

This is typical of the short, stocky privets produced in large numbers in China. The rocks hide a poor root structure. Be suspicious of an excessive amount of rocks and ornaments in the pot.

thick, heavy roots with little space left for fine feeding roots. When repotting, these thick roots should be cut back hard – although not so far that the surface rootage is disfigured – and new feeders will regenerate from around the wound.

What to look for

The vigorous growth means that branches and surface roots may tend to be a little too straight in smaller bonsai. Larger bonsai are less likely to suffer from this problem. Choose an example with natural-looking roots – the branches can be regrown in time if necessary.

Points to watch

All privet are tolerant of dry soil conditions, but they do not take so kindly to having their feet wet for too long. Routine watering in nursery conditions may cause root rot, so check that the tree is firm in its pot before you buy. If the tree is offered for sale indoors or in a greenhouse, it should be in full leaf. Any privet which is kept inside but has lost or is losing leaves is likely to be a sick tree.

LIGUSTRUM SINENSE

BONSAI SOURCES

China, Korea.

LIGHT LEVELS

OUTSIDE **INSIDE**

Full sun (outdoors) or semi- to full shade. If kept in shady conditions indoors, keep temperature fairly low to prevent long, spindly, weak shoots.

TEMPERATURE RANGE

°F -10 0 10 20 30 40 50 60 70 80 90 100

Unaffected by heat if sprayed with clean water. Will tolerate freezing for brief periods, but will lose its leaves. Maximum temperature in winter 68°F.

PESTS AND DISEASES

Scale insects are the biggest danger, but are easily eradicated with systemic insecticide. Mildew and "silver-leaf" fungus can attack plants grown in poor conditions.

SOIL

ORGANIC 60%	GRIT 40%

Repot every two to four years. Cut woody roots back hard.

WATERING

SPRING	SUMMER	FALL	WINTER

Maintain evenly moist soil throughout the year. Never overwater.

FEEDING

SPRING	SUMMER	FALL	WINTER

Low-nitrogen feed throughout the growing season will keep vigor in check and induce flowering.

PRUNING

Trim to shape regularly and thin out cluttered areas as required. Branches can be pruned at any time so long as frost is not expected.

MALUS

Crab apple

HARDY

As soon as flowering has finished, the long shoots must be cut back hard, and the resulting new growth trained to build a framework.

CRAB APPLES ARE grown purely as ornamental trees. The fruits are generally small – sometimes only ¼ inch across – and are unpalatable. The major attraction of *Malus* varieties is the profuse flowering in spring. So many flowers can be borne that the trunk and foliage can become completely obscured by the mass of pink or white blossom.

There are, quite literally, hundreds of varieties of crab apple, but there are only two that are commonly used for commercial bonsai production: *Malus cerasifera* and *M. halliana*, both of which emanate from Japan.

M. cerasifera has mid-green leaves and in spring the pink buds open to fragrant white flowers, up to an inch or so across. The flowers are commonly followed by small, bright red, berry-like fruit hanging on long, slender stalks. The fruit can remain on the tree until some time after the leaves have

turned golden yellow and fallen, giving bonsai of this variety several seasonal high points.

M. halliana rarely produces fruit in significant quantity when grown as a bonsai. However, it has other endearing features. The dark green leaves emerge edged with deep red and, as they mature, the undersides remain this color. The flower buds are deep pink and open to brilliant rich pink flowers no more than ¼ inch across.

All crab apples are very hardy, and can withstand weeks of sub-zero temperatures, but the roots of smaller bonsai should be protected to a certain extent to be safe. Bringing the tree into an unheated but frost-free sun room or greenhouse during the latter part of winter will encourage early flowering, but this shouldn't be done every year as the extended growing season will exhaust the plant after a few years. *Malus* can be brought indoors for brief periods, but cannot be kept indoors permanently.

Since crab apples are grown and pruned for flower production, a tree-like branch structure is less of a criterion than with non-flowering species. But a good branch structure can be developed with care and patience, simply by pruning away inappropriate branches from time to time, and waiting for the "right" ones to develop of their own accord.

To prune for flower production, give the bonsai a general trim to shape immediately following flowering, and then allow all the shoots to grow unchecked until mid- to late summer. Cut back all the shoots to two or three buds. You will notice that the buds, at the base of the shoots, are fatter than those at the tips, because they contain flowers as well as embryonic leaves.

With cheaper bonsai the flowers are the main attraction, but magnificent old specimens like this are superb bonsai in their own right – the blossom is a bonus!

What to look for

It is not necessarily the best time to buy flowering bonsai when in flower. An unhealthy plant may flower well, but die back afterwards. It is far better to buy during midsummer, when the general health of the tree can be assessed. Look for a good, sturdy trunk and branches with many small forks which indicate the existence of flowering spurs.

Points to watch

Crab apples are generally easy to care for, but they do prefer deeper pots with moist soil and plenty of nutrition. An underfed or unhealthy tree may die back or even lose branches after flowering.

MALUS

BONSAI SOURCES

Japan.

LIGHT LEVELS

OUTSIDE   INSIDE

Full sun.

TEMPERATURE RANGE

°F -10 0 10 20 30 40 50 60 70 80 90 100

Constant temperatures in excess of 86°F may cause stress but are unlikely to kill. Withstands temperatures of 15°F. Plants in small containers should have their roots protected in really cold spells.

PESTS AND DISEASES

Aphids and mildew are the most common problems. Apple canker may appear. Affected areas should be cut away entirely.

SOIL

ORGANIC 70%	GRIT 30%

A little clay-based loam may be added. Repot annually in fall. Use a deeper than normal pot to conserve moisture and insulate roots.

WATERING

SPRING	SUMMER	FALL	WINTER

Water well in growing season, especially during fruit formation. Maintain evenly moist during the winter.

FEEDING

SPRING	SUMMER	FALL	WINTER

Balanced feed in spring, low-nitrogen feed from early summer until fall. Finish off with nitrogen-free feed during fall.

PRUNING

Prune branches in fall. Trim to shape in spring, after flowering, then allow unhindered growth. Cut all new shoots back to two or three buds in mid- to late summer.

MURRAYA PANICULATA

Jasmine orange

TENDER

THIS TROPICAL NATIVE of India got its name from its sweet-smelling white flowers which are borne on young shoots, and the small orange fruit which follow. As well as the flowers and fruit, its delicate compound leaves and smooth, pale brown bark have made this species one of the most popular subjects for bonsai in China, where all commercial examples are produced. Being a true tropical, *Murraya* has no dormant season as such in the wild. If grown in more temperate climates, it must be kept indoors from early fall until the last spring frost has passed. During the summer, it will benefit from being allowed to soak up some sun, after being acclimatized by gradually increasing the exposure each day. You can safely leave *Murraya* outdoors at night only in the middle of summer.

In really hot weather, shade the pot to prevent the roots from becoming overheated. It might sound strange that a tropical tree needs protection against the heat, but bear in mind that these are forest trees, whose roots are constantly shaded by the canopy.

Because this species is growing to a certain extent all year round, it prefers a fairly constant supply of water and nutrients. The exact watering and feeding regime will depend on your local conditions. For example, if you live in the northern latitudes, the low light levels in winter will slow the growth almost to a standstill, in spite of the fact that your indoor temperature may be nearly tropical. As a result, the plant will require less water and less feed. If you live further south, the winter light level will be higher, the tree will grow more and will consequently require more water and fertilizer. The trick is to let the

This clump-style *Murraya* specimen is quite old but, nevertheless, the lower branches are being held in position by wire stays. Even old specimen bonsai are constantly in training.

tree tell you what it needs. As growth slows, the soil will remain moist for longer. This is the signal to reduce feed and water. When growth recommences, the soil will dry out quicker, and feed and water should be increased.

If you care for your bonsai well, it will reward you with almost constant flowers followed by fruit which, if sown straight from the tree and kept at 86°F, should germinate and eventually provide you with your own home-grown Indian jungle.

What to look for

Murraya bonsai are generally produced by cutting field-grown trunks down to a foot or so high and training the new shoots as branches. This method can produce ugly scars which should be avoided. Hollow trunks can also result from the heavy surgery. These can be very attractive and are harmless to the tree provided that the decay is arrested before it reaches the roots. Test the tree to ensure it is firm in its pot before buying.

Points to watch

Tropical plants are used to humid conditions, both above and below ground. The foliage looks brighter and healthier if it is sprayed a few times a day, and the roots should never be allowed to dry out. It is a good idea to immerse the pot in a bowl of water once a week to make sure that there are no dry pockets of soil which have been missed by overhead watering.

MURRAYA PANICULATA

BONSAI SOURCES

Southern China.

LIGHT LEVELS

OUTSIDE INSIDE

Full sun or close to a bright window. Shade pot from strong direct sun.

TEMPERATURE RANGE

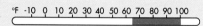

°F -10 0 10 20 30 40 50 60 70 80 90 100

Absolute minimum 54°F for short periods. Ideally, temperatures should not fall below 63°F at any time.

PESTS AND DISEASES

Aphids and red spider mite enjoy the soft new shoots. Mildew can be a problem on trees grown indoors.

SOIL

ORGANIC 70%	GRIT 30%

Repot every two to four years.

WATERING

SPRING	SUMMER	FALL	WINTER
💧💧💧	💧💧💧	💧💧	💧💧

Keep moist at all times. Never let the soil become dry between waterings. Reduce frequency when growth is slower.

FEEDING

SPRING	SUMMER	FALL	WINTER
💧	💧	💧	💧

Weak balanced feed every two weeks throughout the year. If growth slows in winter, reduce frequency by half.

PRUNING

Any time. Bark separates from heartwood easily, so use a sharp tool and cut cleanly.

MYRTUS

Myrtle

HARDY

VARIETIES OF MYRTLE are found in warmer climates throughout the world, from southern Europe through Africa and Asia to South America. However, bonsai of the species are mainly produced in China, and to a lesser extent in Korea and other Far Eastern countries. The prolific white flowers with golden centers, small red to black berries and neat, shiny leaves make very attractive bonsai. Couple these attributes with the species' habit of throwing out vigorous shoots from very old wood, and you have what many Chinese enthusiasts regard as the perfect bonsai material.

If anything, myrtle can be a little too vigorous for the casual bonsai grower. Many adventitious shoots will spring out from all over the trunk and branches and these need to be either pruned away or trained with wire almost on a weekly basis. Although it is possible just to trim the tree to shape like a garden hedge, this practice cannot be relied upon to maintain the tree for more than a few months. The foliage pads will become congested and the more vigorous inner shoots will take over from the older, more desirable branches.

Unlike many other plants from the same regions, *Myrtus* dislikes excessive water in the soil. However,

it does prefer a humid atmosphere so, ironically, it does enjoy being sprayed with cool water as often as possible, all year round.

If you live in a hard water area (where the domestic water supply contains lime or calcium), try to save rainwater to use for both watering and spraying. It is not a strict calcifuge (lime-hater), but it is far happier when growing in slightly acid conditions.

Commercial myrtle bonsai are produced in hundreds of thousands, and are among the cheapest of all to buy. Even very young plants like this can look like little trees. With proper care and attention, there is no reason why this should not develop into a fine bonsai.

Myrtus also requires a dormant period each year. Even if your bonsai has just traveled halfway around the world it will quickly adapt to the new seasonal routine and should be kept fairly cool at 41–50°F with the roots almost dry during the winter months. In summer, it will appreciate fresh air and a little morning sun, but should be shaded during the hottest part of the day.

What to look for

Myrtle bonsai can be produced from pretty old natural material which has either been field grown for the purpose or gathered from the wild. These offer trunks which are full of character and main branches which can form the basis of a fine bonsai. Smaller examples, too, can have interesting trunks, so it is worth spending some time searching for the best of the batch.

Points to watch

Yellowing leaves can be caused by hard water. The lime content locks nutrients in the soil, so the plant effectively becomes starved. This deficiency can be cured in time by repotting in fresh soil and using lime-free water. Check that the nice dense foliage pad is not made up of masses of young adventitious shoots hiding dead old branches.

MYRTUS

BONSAI SOURCES

Bonsai mainly from China.

LIGHT LEVELS

OUTSIDE   INSIDE

Enjoys good light all year round, but must be protected from direct sunlight through glass or hot afternoon sun if kept outdoors.

TEMPERATURE RANGE

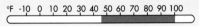

°F -10 0 10 20 30 40 50 60 70 80 90 100

Untroubled by high temperatures if humidity is also high. Keep between 41–50°F during winter. Too high winter temperatures will prevent dormancy and may exhaust the plant.

PESTS AND DISEASES

Aphids attack the young shoots and spider mites invade any congested foliage.

SOIL

ORGANIC 40%	GRIT 60%

Use lime-free or ericaceous compost. Repot every two to three years.

WATERING

SPRING	SUMMER	FALL	WINTER
💧💧	💧💧	💧💧	💧

Keep moist in growing season, but never allow roots to become saturated. Reduce watering to bare minimum in winter. Use soft (lime-free) water or rainwater. Spray daily all year.

FEEDING

SPRING	SUMMER	FALL	WINTER
💧	💧	💧	

Half-strength balanced fertilizer during the growing season. Do not feed in winter.

PRUNING

Pruning can be done at any time, but during the growing season it will promote many new and unwanted shoots. Best done in winter.

NANDINA DOMESTICA

Sacred bamboo

HALF-HARDY

IN SPITE OF its common name, *Nandina* is not a bamboo at all. A native of China and Japan, it is the only species in its genus, and is really a multi-stemmed shrub. Although *Nandina* has become a popular garden plant in temperate zones, where it survives cold winters, it should be regarded as half-hardy when grown in shallow containers.

Nandina is reluctant to produce sturdy branches from the trunk, so it is best to abandon all ideas of producing a tree-like shape. Use the plant's natural habit to create the image of a bamboo grove. The leaf shape and color varies considerably according to the season and even from plant to plant, but, in general, they are long-pointed ovals which emerge bright green tinted with red in spring. In winter, the leaves are not shed, but they frequently turn from copper to bright red, and recover their green color in spring.

The leaves are "pinnate" – composed of several smaller leaflets on a central stalk. If your bonsai begins to look untidy, you can remove up to half of the leaflets by cutting through each central stalk.

Leaves may become scorched by cold wind, so give some shelter in

LEFT
The new foliage emerges deep red, and will retain that color provided it receives good light.

Flowers, fruit, and foliage at the same time are one of the bonuses that *Nandina* has to offer.

winter. *Nandina* are suitable for indoor cultivation provided they can be given cool conditions in winter.

Although *Nandina* does not make sturdy branches, it will throw out a profusion of fine shoots in response to hard pruning. These can quickly form a dense head of foliage, but it will be too open and loose, and disproportionate to the slender trunks. The best way to treat your *Nandina* bonsai is to manage it in much the same way as a Japanese forester might manage a bamboo grove. As each stem becomes too tall or outgrows the design, cut it back almost to ground level. New stems will grow from around the wound as well as from the thicker roots. You can then choose which you want to keep. This constantly changing and developing landscape adds a new dimension to bonsai cultivation which can be as absorbing and rewarding as any single specimen bonsai.

What to look for

Style is irrelevant with *Nandina*. What looks good this week may appear entirely different next week. Choose a plant that is obviously in good health and with as many stems as possible. You can divide the clumps to make several sub-groups in spring.

Points to watch

Some commercial producers export plants that are too young to stand the shock of transportation. They weaken and the roots start to decay. Check that the plant is sturdy and firm in its pot before buying.

Many commercial *Nandina* bonsai are inappropriately planted as single trees, but they are much more valuable in landscape plantings or clumps like this.

NANDINA DOMESTICA

BONSAI SOURCES

China.

LIGHT LEVELS

OUTSIDE   INSIDE

Good overhead light but shaded from direct sun.

TEMPERATURE RANGE

°F -10 0 10 20 30 40 50 60 70 80 90 100

Will withstand light overnight frost, but is best kept above 41°F. In winter, maintain temperatures below 53°F.

PESTS AND DISEASES

Generally trouble-free. Aphids may colonize young shoots.

SOIL

ORGANIC 70%	GRIT 30%

Repot every three to four years. Divide clumps if desired to make new plants.

WATERING

SPRING	SUMMER	FALL	WINTER

Keep moist at all times.

FEEDING

SPRING	SUMMER	FALL	WINTER

Low-nitrogen feed during the growing season. Too much nitrogen in its diet will cause over-sized leaves and leggy growth.

PRUNING

Prune out old stems almost to ground level. Lightly trim side shoots to keep overall shape neat.

OLEA EUROPAEA

European olive
TENDER

OLIVE TREES ARE a familiar sight of the southern European hillsides. Some of them can live for well over a thousand years and adopt grotesque and contorted shapes in their trunks and branches. Their popularity as bonsai was influenced not by the East, but by Israel, where the species' natural readiness to take root from cuttings prompted over-production of young plants. Nowadays, olive bonsai are produced wherever olives grow naturally.

Young olive bonsai are common and very inexpensive, but mature specimens are more rare. The species has not been in use for long enough to develop specimen bonsai from cuttings, and mature-looking trees must be collected from the wild.

There are many varieties or strains of olive that have evolved naturally in different regions. Some have long, narrow leaves, while on others the leaves are almost round. In all cases they are dark, glossy green above, with very pale undersides. Although classed as tender here, olives are very tough and resilient and some strains can stand the occasional nip of frost. However, you can never be certain that your bonsai is one of the more hardy strains, so it is best to treat as fully tender.

Olives are native to dry, arid hillsides, where they can withstand droughts which may literally last for years. In a pot, they also tolerate dry roots for a while, but without the extensive root system they develop in the wild, they will suffer if allowed to remain dry for too long. Olives, like most plants accustomed to dry habitats, are opportunists as far as water consumption is concerned. When water is available, it is taken up at a phenomenal rate, leading the bonsai grower to the false impression that the tree needs liberal watering. It does not.

Pruning olives in spring or early fall will encourage regeneration of

This specimen in the making, with a wonderful gnarled trunk and good branch structure, was collected from open ground and pruned back hard before it was potted. Careful wiring of the young shoots and regular trimming is all that is needed to perfect the image.

This young "starter" tree was grown from a cutting and is good material to build on if you have the patience. The shoots are brittle, so it is best to train by pruning alone until you have become skillful at wiring.

many new, vigorous shoots from all parts of the tree. Pruning when growth is slowest – winter and the hottest part of summer – will result in less regenerative growth.

What to look for
Large specimen olive bonsai are rare and expensive, but offer great charm and character. Younger, more affordable plants should have a single, clear trunk and good basic branch structure. It is more difficult to grow your own branches on olives than on most other species.

Points to watch
Olives are very brittle, so take extreme care when wire training. Olives react unpredictably to the shortening of heavy branches. Rather than produce new shoots from around the wound – as one might expect – the remainder of the branch frequently dies back, and the new shoots emerge from the trunk or even from the roots. It is far better to trim new growth to shape regularly than to allow it to extend and thicken before heavy pruning.

OLEA EUROPAEA

BONSAI SOURCES

Europe, Middle East.

LIGHT LEVELS

Full sun.

OUTSIDE **INSIDE**

TEMPERATURE RANGE

°F -10 0 10 20 30 40 50 60 70 80 90 100

Olives adore hot sun. Temperatures as low as 33°F can be tolerated by some varieties, but a minimum of 41°F should ideally be maintained.

PESTS AND DISEASES

Scale insects and spider mites are the only common problems.

SOIL

ORGANIC 30%	GRIT 70%

Repot every two to three years or even longer. Prune heavy roots back hard, lightly trimming the fine feeding roots.

WATERING

SPRING	SUMMER	FALL	WINTER

Keep slightly on the dry side, watering heavily but infrequently. The colder the temperature, the less water will be required. Spray with clean water during really hot weather.

FEEDING

SPRING	SUMMER	FALL	WINTER

Weak solution of balanced feed throughout the growing season. Top up with nitrogen-free feed in fall. Do not feed in winter.

PRUNING

Prune in spring or early fall. Shortening thick branches may cause remainder of branch to die back, so it is best to do this in small stages rather than in one go.

PICEA

Spruce

HARDY

THERE ARE 50 species of spruce found in the northern temperate regions, and countless varieties, many of them dwarf, which have been bred for use as ornamental garden plants. In spite of this, only one – *Picea glehnii*, Sakhalin spruce – has been developed in Japan for bonsai. Nowadays, it is very difficult to obtain because in most Western countries importation of spruce is tightly controlled for plant health reasons. However, since spruce make fine bonsai which are constantly in demand, home-produced examples using dwarf varieties such as 'Little Gem' or *P. mariana* 'Nana' are becoming increasingly common.

Regardless of the variety, spruce need cold winters in order to thrive, and will die of exhaustion if successive winter temperatures remain above 68°F. All spruce are shallow-rooted, making them ideal for pot cultivation, and are particularly suited to growing in crevices in rocks or on slabs. Forest species tolerate drought for brief periods, but are also generally very thirsty. Dwarf varieties are less tolerant of drought, preferring constantly moist roots.

Spruce have a unique property which requires a specific technique when trimming. The new shoots emerge from the buds looking like tiny green shaving brushes which elongate into a tender shoot clothed with needles. In any other species, pinching out the growing tip would induce new buds to form at the wound and along the shoot. Not with spruce. When severed, a spruce shoot will not produce new buds. It will last until the leaves' useful life is over, and then it will abort. New buds will form, however, at the base of the shoot, and at other intersections. In a healthy tree, buds may form as far back as the trunk.

To trim a spruce, cut all new shoots back to ⅛–¼ inch as soon as the needles have begun to stand at right angles to the shoot. By midsummer, new buds will begin to open in the locations described above. These resulting shoots will be very short and may be left untrimmed. Every three or four

Thinning the foliage creates space between the branches which makes the tree look bigger and older.

Spruce develop wonderfully uniform, compact foliage with regular pinching of new shoots. Every few years, it is necessary to thin out congested areas to allow light and air to penetrate.

years, the old, worn-out, pruned shoots must be cut out, and congested areas thinned to allow light and air to penetrate the inner areas, thus stimulating yet more back budding.

What to look for

Dwarf spruce are often sold as rock-plantings, whereas Sakhalin spruce are most commonly used for forest-style bonsai. The most important factor to consider is the shape. A spruce bonsai should look like an old conifer. Unfortunately, many home-producers tend to make them look like apple trees, which just won't do! Avoid trees with yellowing foliage, which could indicate the presence of aphids or spider mite.

Points to watch

Spruce suffer badly from attacks by red spider mites and tiny spruce aphids, especially when sheltered during winter. Congested foliage and poor air circulation can exacerbate the problem, and both these conditions are common in commercial nurseries. Infestations are easily eliminated with a brand garden insecticide, but it would be foolish to buy an infested bonsai and introduce a new pest to the rest of your collection.

PICEA

BONSAI SOURCES

Japan.

LIGHT LEVELS

OUTSIDE   INSIDE

Will tolerate full sun throughout the summer in temperate zones. In warmer climates, some shade is necessary. Can be kept in deep shade in winter.

TEMPERATURE RANGE

°F -10 0 10 20 30 40 50 60 70 80 90 100

Must have periods during the winter when temperatures are near freezing or below to remain in good health, although smaller trees should be protected from profound freezing. In warmer climates, place spruce in the shadiest part of your yard during winter.

PESTS AND DISEASES

Aphids and red spider mites are common. Adelgids may cause pineapple-like galls on shoots. Two types of rust can occur, but are usually only temporary conditions.

SOIL

ORGANIC **70%**	GRIT **30%**

Repot every two to three years. Trees on rocks should have wedges of old soil removed and replaced with fresh, rather than being removed from the rock.

WATERING

SPRING	SUMMER	FALL	WINTER
🌢🌢🌢	🌢🌢🌢	🌢🌢🌢	🌢🌢

Maintain high moisture levels at all times, but avoid waterlogging, especially in winter.

FEEDING

SPRING	SUMMER	FALL	WINTER
🌢	🌢	🌢	

Balanced feed until late summer. Nitrogen-free feed until fall.

PRUNING

Prune branches in fall, when wounds will "bleed" less resin. Trim new shoots hard in spring, but leave second flush untrimmed.

PINUS DENSIFLORA

Red pine

HARDY

THE RAREST OF the three Japanese pines, but nonetheless highly prized for its flaky bark and shiny, bright green needles. Red pine is slow-growing, so bonsai take a long time to develop, which accounts for its rarity and corresponding high price.

The maintenance trimming of two-needled pines (red pine and black pine, *Pinus thunbergii*) involves a carefully timed cycle of pinching and pruning during the growing season, which is based on the trees' annual growth cycle. In spring, the buds do not open in the same way as other species; they gradually elongate, as tiny needles appear, pressed tight to the central shoot. As the elongation of these "candles" continues, the needles grow and begin to peel away from the shoot. Eventually, they become full-size and stand more or less at right angles to the shoot, and a cluster of buds appears at the tip.

The pinching process consists of simply breaking off each extending candle before it reaches maturity. However, by adjusting the timing of the exercise, very different results are achieved:

• To strengthen weak branches and build up dense foliage. When the needles begin to extend but before they separate from the shoot, break off about two-thirds of the candle. By the end of the summer, two or

three buds will have formed at the broken-off end, and one or two others at the base of the shoot. Cover the whole tree, spreading the work over a period of a week or more. Begin at the weakest part and finish at the strongest.

• To extend branches. Allow the candle to extend until it reaches the desired length. Ideally, the needles should by now be standing away from the shoot, but only about a third of their full size. Break off about a quarter of the candle. One or two new buds will form at the tip and also at the base of the shoot. Next year, follow the technique to build up foliage outlined above.

• To encourage back budding. By the middle of summer, the shoots should be almost mature. Buds will have formed at the tips and the needles will be almost full size but paler green. Shorten the shoot, leaving just a few pairs of needles. This rather drastic treatment prompts the production of large numbers of buds on all parts of the branch by the following summer. Once these buds have sprouted, older branches can be removed if desired.

Older needles should be routinely plucked out in late summer, taking care to leave any pairs of needles that have a minute developing bud between them.

If the needles seem to be too long in proportion to the shape of the tree, they can easily be reduced by following the technique outlined under black pine on page 129.

What to look for
Red pine are traditionally grown in the slender "literati" style, which exposes the attractive bark. The trunk should have an interesting shape, and should taper gradually from base to tip.

Points to watch
The flaky bark takes a long time to develop, so consider this when buying a young plant. Also, check carefully that there are no unsightly wire marks, which can take many years to heal.

The exact age of this priceless specimen is uncertain, but it has a recorded history going back centuries. It is currently in the American National Collection.

PINUS DENSIFLORA

BONSAI SOURCES

Japan.

LIGHT LEVELS

OUTSIDE — INSIDE

Full sun.
Very small pots should not be allowed to overheat.

TEMPERATURE RANGE

°F -10 0 10 20 30 40 50 60 70 80 90 100
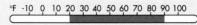

Prefers a period of freezing conditions to harden off foliage and to induce semi-dormancy. Cannot be kept indoors.

PESTS AND DISEASES

 Woolly aphids, mealy bugs, adelgids and other undesirables enjoy the sap-rich shoots and needles. Use a systemic insecticide with a drop of detergent in the water to help penetrate the insects' waxy coating.

SOIL

ORGANIC 30%	GRIT 70%

Excellent drainage is essential. Repot annually for young trees, every three to four years for older specimens.

WATERING

SPRING	SUMMER	FALL	WINTER
🌢🌢🌢	🌢🌢	🌢🌢	🌢🌢

Keep moist, but try to avoid soil becoming saturated for too long. Control watering to reduce needle length if required (see page 128).

FEEDING

SPRING	SUMMER	FALL	WINTER
🌢	🌢	🌢	

 Weak balanced feed until late summer. Weak low-nitrogen until the end of fall. Increase the frequency of feeding for developing trees. A light dressing of bonemeal in early winter will benefit the tree in the following spring.

PRUNING

Pinch candles before they mature. Prune branches in late summer when sap is falling.

PINUS PARVIFLORA

White pine

HARDY

THIS RATHER "FEMININE" looking species is regarded as the queen of all pines. Its needles, which are borne in groups of five (another botanical name for white pine is *P. pentaphylla* – five-leaved), are bluish-green below and blue-white above. The shoots, too, are blue-white, giving the whole tree a silvery, almost distant appearance.

White pines have a smooth bark, even on very mature trees. To make more attractive bonsai, white pines are invariably grafted onto trunks of black pine (*P. thunbergii*), whose heavily fissured bark is far more desirable. The graft union will always be visible, so it has to be disguised somehow. To do this, the first branch is grown immediately above the graft and trained so that the foliage covers the point of union.

The dense tufts of needles, so characteristic of white pine, conceal a mass of buds at the tip of each shoot which can quickly form heavy foliage masses. These can become congested and overgrown within a few years, making it necessary to

prune back the branch tips to convenient inner growth every few years. This remaining inner growth can be wire-trained to replace the areas that have been removed.

Summer pinching is easy. As the shoots extend, they can simply be pinched off between finger and thumb, taking care not to break any individual needles. Remove about half the length of each shoot, starting the process on the bottom branch and finishing a week or so later at the apex.

If lower branches appear weak, this is because the tree's natural tendency is to direct most of its energy to the apex in order to gain height. This energy can be redirected by reducing the amount of foliage in the stronger-growing parts. Do this by plucking out older needles individually. Leave four or five clusters in the most vigorous parts of the tree, increasing the amount remaining on weaker branches, and leaving the weakest of all untouched. Within a couple of years, this treatment should redress any imbalance.

As a matter of course, old, jaded needles should be cleaned out periodically in order to allow light and air to penetrate inner areas.

FAR LEFT
This inexpensive white pine has all the attributes of a good basic bonsai: an interesting trunk, fairly well-placed branches, and healthy foliage. A specimen just waiting to be developed!

BELOW
Careful wiring of the young shoots and regular pinching will improve the somewhat loose appearance of this semi-specimen white pine.

What to look for

Avoid white pine bonsai grown from seed as the bark will always remain smooth and boring, and the plant will be slow to develop. Ensure that the graft union is reasonably unobtrusive and hidden behind a thoughtfully positioned branch.

Points to watch

All pines do best in well-drained soil and rapidly deteriorate in wet or waterlogged conditions. Although fully hardy, white pines can suffer in severe winters, so giving some protection against drying cold winds and prolonged heavy freezing is advisable.

The uncomfortable space at the top right of the tree should be filled by training a new branch into position, possibly using one from the rear of the tree.

The strong trunk and root spread justify the higher price of this tree. The branches have already been trained into position, ready for its new owner to develop the foliage clouds.

PINUS PARVIFLORA

BONSAI SOURCES

Japan.

LIGHT LEVELS

OUTSIDE   INSIDE

Full sun or partial shade.
Color is better and needles are shorter when grown in full sun.

TEMPERATURE RANGE

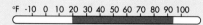

°F -10 0 10 20 30 40 50 60 70 80 90 100

Protect from prolonged spells below 22°F. Do not keep indoors for more than a day or so at any time of year.

PESTS AND DISEASES

Aphids, scale insects. Root aphids may debilitate the tree. Check for these regularly and drench the soil with insecticide at first sight.

SOIL

ORGANIC 30%	GRIT 70%

Repot young plants every two years and older established trees every four to five years. Delay repotting until late spring.

WATERING

SPRING	SUMMER	FALL	WINTER
🌢🌢🌢	🌢🌢🌢	🌢🌢	🌢

Keep moist but not wet. White pine suffers more from overwatering than from drought, so some overhead shelter during prolonged rainy spells is advisable.

FEEDING

SPRING	SUMMER	FALL	WINTER
🌢	🌢	🌢	

Weak balanced feed throughout the growing season, nitrogen-free from fall until early winter.

PRUNING

Pinch off tips of shoots to maintain shape. Thin congested areas every two to three years. Prune branches in late summer to fall.

PINUS THUNBERGII

Black pine
HARDY

IF *P. PARVIFLORA* IS the queen of pines, then this must surely be the king. The black pine's dark, craggy bark and deep, shiny green needles, which always seem to stand erect, develop into a strong, very masculine tree. In Japan, it is said that the newcomers to bonsai are enchanted by the white pine's delicate coloration, but the connoisseur prefers the strength and durability of the black pine.

Indeed, in Japan, the black pine is a common street and park tree, selected for its tolerance to poor soil and dry conditions and its wonderfully obliging response to pruning. Nearly every street and parkland pine in Japan is routinely pruned and shaped by hand every year or two, and the sight of these "giant bonsai" is breathtaking for the Western visitor.

Most black pine bonsai exported from Japan will be grown in the formal or informal upright styles, resulting in squat, triangular shapes. These styles are easy to maintain once established on medium to large bonsai, but are more difficult to maintain on smaller trees because of the needle length. Smaller bonsai need to be much simpler in structure in order to be successful.

Although the needles on black pine are long, there is a very useful technique that can be employed which will reduce the size of any given annual crop of foliage. This technique is also suitable for red pine.

• In spring, allow the "candles" to extend and pinch them back in the normal way.

• The needles reach the ideal length – say ¼–1 inch long – before either they or the shoot have fully matured. As soon as they reach this length, withhold water, allowing the soil to become virtually (but not completely) dry.

• As long as the soil is kept almost dry, the needles will cease to grow any longer.

• By midsummer, the needles will "harden off." The color will darken and they will stand erect from the shoot. At this point, normal watering can be resumed, and the needles will not grow any longer.

Keep in mind that this will only affect the current year's crop of needles. The process has to be repeated every year to maintain uniform needle length.

The summer pinching and trimming routine is very straightforward, and can be modified according to the results you want to achieve. For a full description of the techniques, see red pine (page 124).

What to look for
Black pine grows fairly quickly, and some bonsai can have long immature branches with little character. It is always worth looking for a specimen with a good, craggy trunk and branches. Black pine bonsai are generally grown from seed, so there is no excuse for yours not having a well-formed surface root structure.

Points to watch
Overwatering is probably the biggest risk. Too much water will turn the needles yellow, reduce back budding and rot the roots. Check the soil every day, and only water the tree if there are signs of dryness (unless you are employing the needle-reduction technique). Be especially careful in the wet winter months. Although fully hardy, the roots may suffer if frozen for long periods. Recently pruned branches may also suffer from dieback if exposed to frost too soon after pruning.

This style is called a "raft." The three trunks were originally low branches which were trained sideways before being allowed to grow vertically. The original central trunk was then removed entirely.

PINUS THUNBERGII

BONSAI SOURCES

Japan.

LIGHT LEVELS

OUTSIDE   INSIDE

Full sun.
Tolerates a little shade but color and sturdiness will suffer.

TEMPERATURE RANGE

°F -10 0 10 20 30 40 50 60 70 80 90 100
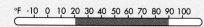

Requires a period of cold in winter to allow the tree to rest, but some protection against prolonged freezing is advisable.

PESTS AND DISEASES

 Woolly aphids, mealy bugs, adelgids and other undesirables enjoy the sap-rich shoots and needles. Use a systemic insecticide with a drop of detergent in the water to help penetrate the insects' waxy coating.

SOIL

ORGANIC 20%	GRIT 80%

Connoisseurs use 100% grit, but a careful daily check on moisture content must be made. Repot young trees every two years, older trees up to every five years, depending on root growth.

WATERING

SPRING	SUMMER	FALL	WINTER
💧💧	💧💧	💧💧	💧

Black pines are drought tolerant, but dislike waterlogged soil. Water thoroughly, but only when the soil begins to show signs of drought. Give less water in winter.

FEEDING

SPRING	SUMMER	FALL	WINTER
💧	💧	💧	

Balanced fertilizer from spring to the end of summer. Low-nitrogen in fall and early winter.

PRUNING

Pinch new shoots to maintain compact foliage. Thin out congested areas every two years in late summer. Prune branches in late summer, early fall.

PISTACIA TEREBINTHUS

Pistachio

TENDER

THIS SUBTROPICAL EVERGREEN tree is native to the Far East and the Mediterranean region. It has dark, glossy green leaves which are "pinnate;" this means that each leaf is composed of several smaller leaflets grouped in pairs along a central stalk.

On a bonsai, each pinnate leaf can actually appear like a shoot with individual leaves growing from it. This can be utilized on small bonsai, but only as a temporary measure. Bear in mind that all leaves have a limited useful life, and when this is over, the leaf is shed – on evergreens as well as deciduous species. When a small bonsai sheds a pinnate leaf, it is visually losing a branch, which can significantly change its shape. Similarly, when a new shoot emerges, with two or three new leaves, it can create the impression of a whole new branch formation.

For this reason, it is much better to set your sights on a medium to large size pistachio bonsai, rather than a small one which will always present these problems of scale. However, if you do go for a smaller tree, you can compromise by shortening the leaves. To do this, cut through the central stalk, removing all but one pair of leaflets. This action will encourage new growth, so unless you particularly want to encourage new

growth in specific areas, it is best to reduce the leaves evenly all over the tree in this way.

Pistachios tend to thicken very significantly in the early part of the growing season, during which time the branches can be pretty brittle as they are pumped full of sap. If you want to wire-train your bonsai, wait until towards the end of the growing season, when the branches will be more supple and less likely to snap.

Although natives of fairly dry, arid regions, pistachios are surprisingly thirsty. In nature, their extensive root system penetrates deep into the ground to maintain a good supply of water. However, in a pot, this is clearly impossible. As a result, pistachios are susceptible to problems associated with dry roots: mildew, premature leaf fall, dieback, etc. The solution is to use a

Pistacias have compound leaves, made up from several pairs of leaflets, which can look untidy on small bonsai. To keep the outline neat, you can cut through the central stem of each leaf, leaving only one or two pairs of leaflets.

This budget-priced example has a good, sturdy trunk with interesting movement and could develop into a worthwhile bonsai.

standard, well-drained soil, but to cover the surface with moss or flat pebbles to prevent evaporation. A localized humid atmosphere and regular spraying of the foliage with water also helps.

What to look for

Because of their pinnate leaves, pistachios are best when trained as larger bonsai. However, they do make attractive group plantings, particularly when incorporated with rocks and mosses to form miniature landscapes. Choose an example with trunks of varying height and thicknesses, and ensure they have healthy roots by gently rocking them – they should feel firm.

Points to watch

The leaves are the best indicator of a plant's health. On pistachio, they will turn yellow if all is not well, particularly if the roots are unhappy. The soil must be kept well moistened but not wet, and never allowed either to dry out or to become waterlogged.

Cold drafts will also cause foliage, and even the young shoots, to perish.

PISTACIA TEREBINTHUS

BONSAI SOURCES

China, Korea, other Far Eastern countries.

LIGHT LEVELS

OUTSIDE   INSIDE

Bright, but protected from full sun through glass. If grown outside, provide shade during the hottest part of the day only.

TEMPERATURE RANGE

°F -10 0 10 20 30 40 50 60 70 80 90 100

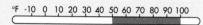

Will survive temperatures as low as 41°F for brief periods, but is best kept above 50°F.

PESTS AND DISEASES

Scale insects, spider mites and woolly aphids can cause problems. Root rot and microscopic systemic fungi can cause trees to collapse. There is no effective cure for these, but good growing conditions and hygiene will prevent them occurring.

SOIL

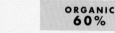

ORGANIC 60%	GRIT 40%

Repot every three years unless it becomes potbound before then.

WATERING

SPRING	SUMMER	FALL	WINTER
🌢🌢🌢	🌢🌢🌢	🌢🌢	🌢🌢

Keep soil moist at all times. Do not allow soil to become dry or waterlogged. Spray daily with clean water.

FEEDING

SPRING	SUMMER	FALL	WINTER
🌢	🌢	🌢	

Balanced feed throughout the growing season. If temperatures remain above 68°F during winter, a weak feed can be given every three to four weeks at that time.

PRUNING

Prune branches at any time of year. Use sharp tools as the bark separates from the wood easily if clumsily pruned. Leaves may be reduced to one pair of leaflets if desired.

PODOCARPUS MACROPHYLLUS

Plum-fruited/Chinese yew
HALF-HARDY

THIS CONIFEROUS EVERGREEN is one of the most popular ornamental garden trees in its native China and Japan, although only the Chinese commonly use the species for bonsai cultivation. It is thought that the reason is that the Japanese prefer the more easily controllable, finer foliage of the similar yew *Taxus cuspidata* (see page 150).

The natural habit of *Podocarpus* is for the trunk to divide into several vertical branches at a yard or two high. This tendency is apparent when grown on a smaller scale. Even though the branches on a bonsai may be wired to below the horizontal, the shoots that grow from them will have a strong vertical thrust that needs to be controlled by hard pruning.

Podocarpus respond well to pruning by throwing out many side shoots from new and old wood alike. However, they are slow-growing, so commercial producers tend to rely on the mass of dark green, closely packed leaves to provide visual bulk, rather than a well-structured branch.

In extreme cases, the slender trunks of young specimens are looped and twisted into the most bizarre shapes in an attempt to create a tree-shaped blob of green foliage on a stick. This silliness is not bonsai. It is simply a cynical trick by unscrupulous commercial

The naturally occurring twin trunks of this clump-style *Podocarpus* form a stable base for the heavy foliage mass above it.

The foliage on *Podocarpus* can rapidly become untidy as the tree grows. Regular pinching of the growing tips will reduce the size of the leaves to a certain extent, and cutting away all the downward-facing leaves keeps the foliage clouds neat.

producers to exploit the uneducated Western public. The Western retailers who sell the trees are not to blame, as they rarely see them until they are delivered.

When grown in open ground, *Podocarpus* is regarded as fully hardy, but it has been known to die back to the base in really severe winters. In a pot, the roots also become less able to tolerate freezing, so *Podocarpus* bonsai are regarded as half-hardy. They benefit from being allowed to live outside during the summer in temperate regions, provided they are given some protection from full sun during the hottest part of the day. But they should be protected from frosts that are heavy enough to threaten to freeze the soil.

What to look for

Search for an example that has a thick, undivided trunk with established branches. These may be rare and a little more expensive than some of the more eccentrically shaped offerings, but are worth the additional cost.

Points to watch

Podocarpus do not like having their roots pruned, and can "sulk" if it is overdone. The roots may die back further, causing loss of foliage and branches. In extreme cases, the entire tree may collapse. When repotting, be careful not to cut away more than about one eighth of the root mass, and keep soil only just moist until new growth has begun. Too much water following root pruning may cause the roots to rot.

PODOCARPUS MACROPHYLLUS

BONSAI SOURCES

China.

LIGHT LEVELS

Outside: full sun, protect from very hot sun. Indoors: bright position, but away from direct sun.

TEMPERATURE RANGE

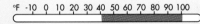
°F -10 0 10 20 30 40 50 60 70 80 90 100

Minimum 41°F during winter. Can tolerate brief light frosts, but it is best not to take this for granted.

PESTS AND DISEASES

Scale insects, red spider mites and mealy bugs are regular visitors. Mildew may occur in plants with dry roots and overcrowded foliage.

SOIL

ORGANIC 60%	GRIT 40%

Repot every three years. Do not remove more than one eighth of the root mass. Use sharp tools.

WATERING

SPRING	SUMMER	FALL	WINTER
🌢🌢🌢	🌢🌢🌢	🌢🌢🌢	🌢🌢

Keep moist at all times during growing season. Reduce water slightly in winter, depending on temperature. Spray regularly in hot weather.

FEEDING

SPRING	SUMMER	FALL	WINTER
🌢	🌢	🌢	🌢

Weak balanced feed whenever the tree is growing. If it is kept in warm conditions in winter, it will continue growing all year round, and so will still require some nutrients.

PRUNING

Prune branches at any time. Encourage side growth by cutting through new shoots with sharp scissors. The fibrous stems will split and crush if blunt tools are used.

PRUNUS MUME

Japanese flowering apricot

HARDY

THE *PRUNUS* GENUS includes over 400 species of trees and shrubs which include ornamental and fruiting varieties of almonds, cherries, plums, peaches and evergreen laurels, along with their countless hybrids. *Prunus mume* falls within the "plum" category.

The Japanese apricot must be one of the most familiar elements in Japanese art and decoration. The delicate, fragrant white to pale pink flowers, clasping to bare, dark and craggy twigs in late winter, are symbolic of nature's strength and beauty. It is the contrast between the gnarled flowering spurs and the delicate blossom, the flimsy petals withstanding wind, rain and even snow, that has influenced the bonsai artist as well.

Large specimen bonsai are rare and even more rarely leave Japan. They are mostly *yamadori* or collected from the mountains, already old and full of character, and very expensive! They invariably have heavy, hollow trunks with gnarled bark and some areas of carved dead wood imitating lightning strikes. The few branches are sharply bent and taper dramatically to a small number of flower-bearing twigs.

The principle is to create the most rugged framework possible for the fragile flowers.

After flowering, the shoots are allowed to grow untrimmed to enable healthy flower buds to develop for next spring. The shoots will be trimmed back hard in late summer. Specimen bonsai like this one normally display heavy, gnarled trunks.

Fortunately, commercial growers had the foresight some years ago to begin the long process of commercial production. We can now reap the benefit as good quality, small- to medium-sized bonsai have become readily available. They consist of short, stumpy trunks with sparse, heavily pruned branches. They also inevitably have many ugly scars. These you will have to carve out to form natural-looking hollows, possibly enlarging them as time goes by. Thus you develop the gnarled trunk. The branch shapes will almost take care of themselves. They are largely the result of the pruning technique employed designed to encourage flowering.

The pruning technique is really quite simple.

• Immediately after flowering, cut back hard. Last year's growth can be shortened to one or two buds, or removed completely if it spoils the branch line. Prune out old, overgrown spurs and too long branches at this time as well.

• Allow unrestricted growth all summer. Next spring's flower buds will form in the axils of the buds towards the base of most shoots. By the end of summer, they will appear slightly rounder than the growth buds further along the shoot.

• In fall, clip all shoots back to three to five buds.

You will soon discover how easy it is to develop those craggy branches.

What to look for

Don't expect to find a work of art. Look for a tree with "potential." A good root formation, tapered trunk and well-spaced branches are the criteria. Buy when the tree is in flower so you can approve the color.

Points to watch

Although fully hardy, the flowers can suffer from sharp frosts. Wild Japanese apricots have their roots well insulated deep in volcanic soil, so they need protection from severe freezing when grown in small pots. Place the tree in a garage or shed during cold spells.

Even young, relatively undeveloped trees bear masses of delightful blossoms in early spring. These can vary from deep pink to creamy white.

PRUNUS MUME

BONSAI SOURCES

China, Japan.

LIGHT LEVELS

OUTSIDE   INSIDE

Full sun.
Not suitable for indoors.

TEMPERATURE RANGE

°F -10 0 10 20 30 40 50 60 70 80 90 100

Provide some shade in very hot weather. Tolerates freezing for brief periods. Frost may damage flowers.

PESTS AND DISEASES

Aphids are inevitable. Spray every two weeks as a precaution. Occasional scale insects. Mildew can damage shoots in poor conditions. Various cankers can damage branches – cut the affected branch back to healthy wood as soon as diagnosed.

SOIL

ORGANIC 60%	GRIT 40%

A little loam could be added. Use a deepish pot. Repot every year immediately after flowering. Less often for older plants.

WATERING

SPRING	SUMMER	FALL	WINTER

Water well in spring and summer, keep soil moist but not wet in winter. Note: as the flower buds swell, the demand for water increases. Allowing the soil to dry at this stage will cause the buds to drop.

FEEDING

SPRING	SUMMER	FALL	WINTER

Balanced fertilizer in spring, frequent low-nitrogen feeds in summer and nitrogen-free in fall.

PRUNING

Prune hard after flowering (delay for three weeks after repotting), trim again in fall.

PSEUDOCYDONIA SINENSIS

Chinese quince

HARDY

CHINESE QUINCE IS much more of a tree than its distant relation, the shrubby Japanese quince. It is also much more successful as a species for specimen bonsai. Ironically, although not indigenous to Japan, it is there, rather than China, that *Pseudocydonia* made it into the big time in bonsai.

Although the small, pink flowers are reason enough to want a Chinese quince bonsai, in Japan it is the winter image of this tree that is particularly appreciated. Its smooth, pale buff bark peels away in thin, irregular patches, revealing tints of ochre, pink and green. The pattern this creates is constantly changing in form and in color. The branches become heavy, tapered and gnarled through years of pruning to encourage flowering and fruiting. In fine specimens, the pattern on the trunk is continued along the branches.

The yellow fruits, which are disproportionately large, are traditionally treated in a rather bizarre fashion. All but three fruits are removed in early summer. When ripe, the remaining ones are carefully repositioned by impaling them on specially selected short twigs. This practice might seem a little curious to Westerners, but in Japan, the subtle positioning of the fruits is an art in itself! My favorite story suggests that it is done to signify the three moons of winter. Whatever the reason, the result is stunning.

Your Chinese quince is likely to be a little more modest. If you are lucky, it will already be mature enough to flower. However, before you concern yourself too much with flowers, you have to build up a strong framework of branches.

The deep pot encourages rapid development and prolific flowering. For the next few years, while the tree is in training, the flower buds should be removed to divert energy into growth.

Established Chinese quince bonsai are rare and extremely expensive, so this is the type of offering you can expect to find in commercial nurseries. Once the flowers have faded, training can begin in earnest.

Hard pruning in early spring will encourage vigorous new shoots which should be wire-trained immediately, before they become brittle. Cutting these back by half in midsummer will encourage a second flush of side shoots which must also be wired sideways. Once you have achieved a satisfactory branch framework, you can prune for flowers.

To encourage flowering and fruiting, allow all new shoots to grow freely until late summer, when they can be cut back to two or three leaves, and give plenty of low-nitrogen fertilizer – the maximum recommended by the manufacturer. Further heavy pruning should be done in fall.

What to look for

Because this species is appreciated in winter, it is important that the bark is not blemished with bad scars. Look for a smooth, gently curving trunk line that continues as far into the crown as possible. Branches can easily be pruned and regrown if necessary. Study the possibilities of changing the viewing angle to hide scars and improve the trunk line.

Points to watch

Branches and even year-old shoots are annoyingly brittle, so it is best to prune and regrow rather than wire them. Young shoots set in position quickly – cut off the wire before it constricts the shoot. Remove all but a few fruits to conserve the tree's energy and to increase the size of the remaining ones.

PSEUDOCYDONIA SINENSIS

BONSAI SOURCES

Most bonsai from Japan.

LIGHT LEVELS

OUTSIDE   INSIDE

Full sun.
Give shade to small pots in hot weather.

TEMPERATURE RANGE

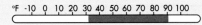

°F -10 0 10 20 30 40 50 60 70 80 90 100

Requires a cold winter dormant period. Tolerates light frost, but should not be allowed to become frozen solid.

PESTS AND DISEASES

Aphids, scale insects, mildew – all easily rectified.

SOIL

ORGANIC	GRIT
60%	40%

Japanese Akadama clay is also good. Repot every two to three years in fall. Use an ample pot.

WATERING

SPRING	SUMMER	FALL	WINTER

Water well in growing season and while fruit are swelling. Keep just moist in winter.

FEEDING

SPRING	SUMMER	FALL	WINTER

Frequent low-nitrogen feeds in summer, nitrogen-free in fall.

PRUNING

Branch pruning in fall. Trim the shoots back to two or three leaves in the late summer.

PUNICA GRANATUM

Pomegranate

TENDER

MUCH LOVED BY the Romans, who were responsible for its spread to all parts of the Mediterranean region, the pomegranate is also native from southern China to India. It seldom grows to more than a large shrub and is cultivated for its red, pink or white flowers, and succulent fruit.

Pomegranate is semi-deciduous. This means that although it requires a rest period during the winter, it does not need to shut down completely. Its metabolism can continue to function slowly, provided the temperature remains sufficiently high.

For instance, if winter temperatures remain around 64–68°F, some leaves may be retained, and those that fall will quickly be replaced. On the other hand, if temperatures fall to 41–45°F, the leaves will soon fall and will not be replaced until spring. This will also affect the watering regime. When the tree is in leaf, it will require more water, not only to sustain the foliage and growth, but also because the warmer temperatures encourage faster evaporation. As temperatures fall, so does the demand for water.

Apart from the flowers, the pomegranate's most endearing feature is the characteristic texture of the bark. As the pale gray to buff bark matures, it adopts a wrinkled

texture. The main vascular lines between roots and main branches become enlarged and the spaces between them shrink, imparting to the trunk a sinuous, often twisted shape. As time passes, the shrunken areas die and decay, causing splits and hollows to occur, which all add to the tree's apparent age. This natural process creates an almost exact miniature replica of an ancient, full-sized pomegranate.

The roots of this little pomegranate are not in contact with the rock, whereas they should clasp it tightly. It would take several years of healthy growth to improve this flaw.

Even though this pomegranate is fairly young, it is already bearing flowers and ripening fruit, and has a very believable tree-like shape.

Pomegranates like plenty of water, preferring fertile valleys to arid mountains. When the fruits are ripening, their demand is even higher, so you will need to modify the amount of water according to the tree's needs. Close observation will teach you to read the signs.

What to look for

If possible, buy your pomegranate when it is in flower, so you can be sure of the color. Choose a tree whose roots are spread widely and evenly around the base of the trunk. The trunk itself should not be ramrod-straight. A curved trunk will improve with age; a straight one will always be boring.

Points to watch

Pomegranates flower on short shoots growing from last year's wood. Be careful not to trim these off when pruning. Branches can be very brittle, so wire training should be carried out when shoots are still green and pliable. Give plenty of water while flower buds and fruit are swelling to avoid failure.

PUNICA GRANATUM

BONSAI SOURCES

Mediterranean, India, China.

LIGHT LEVELS

OUTSIDE   INSIDE

Full sun.
Will tolerate sun through a window if the pot is kept in shade.

TEMPERATURE RANGE

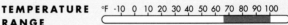

°F -10 0 10 20 30 40 50 60 70 80 90 100

Minimum of 64°F to remain evergreen, deciduous or semi-deciduous below this. Absolute minimum of 41°F. May be placed outdoors in full sun during summer in temperate zones.

PESTS AND DISEASES

Most garden pests will attack pomegranate, so a regular precautionary spray with systemic insecticide is recommended. Yellowing leaves may indicate too much lime in the soil or water.

SOIL

ORGANIC 50%	GRIT 50%

Repot every two years, older plants less frequently. Early spring is the best time, before the new growth is under way.

WATERING

SPRING	SUMMER	FALL	WINTER

Keep moist at all times, using rainwater as far as possible. Water prolifically when flower buds and fruit are swelling. Reduce water to a minimum if leaves fall.

FEEDING

SPRING	SUMMER	FALL	WINTER

Balanced feed until flowering. Low-nitrogen feed late summer and fall. If in leaf in winter, give an occasional low-nitrogen feed at half strength.

PRUNING

Heavy pruning is best immediately following flowering. Allow shoots to extend to five or six leaves, then cut back to two. Do not prune non-extending, flowering shoots.

PYRACANTHA

Firethorn

HARDY/TENDER

A PROFUSION OF tiny, creamy-white flowers borne in wide pannicles, followed by masses of crimson, orange or yellow berries, make this shrub one of the most popular plants in the West. Its vigorous response to pruning and its sharp spines make it ideal for boundary hedging. The former is also an asset when growing *Pyracantha* as bonsai; the latter is not as it can make wire training an extremely painful process!

Although originally from China, it was the Japanese who pioneered the use of this species as material for bonsai. Its drawbacks are that the trunks are slow to thicken and that the branches are stiff and easily broken when being wire-trained. The first problem is often solved by planting the tree with its roots clasping a rock as they grow down into the soil, which creates a visually strong base.

Other popular styles are semi- and full-cascade. Opting for this style reduces the need for such a thick trunk, and allows the large clusters of flowers and berries plenty of room to develop. The branches are shaped by pruning alone, which is, in turn, dictated by the need to encourage and accommodate the flowers and fruit.

If you look closely, you will see that the spines are really short shoots that have become hard at the tip. The longer of these spines, which grow in all directions, protect next year's flower buds. These appear on short shoots that grow from the side of spines.

In spring, cut back to a spine that is growing in roughly the direction you want the flowering shoot to grow, and eliminate any that grow inwards. Remember to leave plenty of space between each branch and the one above it. This is important because the flowers are generally raised above the branch, but the berries hang below it, so extra space must be allowed. Longer extension shoots should be wired early and pruned hard in fall to encourage more side growth.

All *Pyracantha* bonsai from Japan are hardy, but some tropical species from the Philippines are on the

This young *Pyracantha* is typical of the inexpensive smaller trees available. It would benefit from being allowed to grow unchecked for a few years until it is big enough to accommodate the panicles of flowers without them appearing too large for the tree.

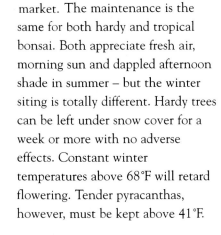

The sturdy trunk of this specimen *Pyracantha* is a perfect counterfoil to the masses of fragrant, creamy-white flowers and later the bright orange-red berries.

market. The maintenance is the same for both hardy and tropical bonsai. Both appreciate fresh air, morning sun and dappled afternoon shade in summer – but the winter siting is totally different. Hardy trees can be left under snow cover for a week or more with no adverse effects. Constant winter temperatures above 68°F will retard flowering. Tender pyracanthas, however, must be kept above 41°F.

What to look for

Choose your *Pyracantha* while it is bearing fruit. The color varies considerably from plant to plant. With root-over-rock styles, ensure that the roots clasp the rock tightly. Cascades should bend sharply over the rim of the pot – a smooth curve is unnatural and boring. Check whether you are buying a hardy or tender species.

Points to watch

The spines are very sharp and can cause serious pain. It is not a bad idea to snip the tips off before wiring.

PYRACANTHA

BONSAI SOURCES

China, Japan. Tropicals from Philippines.

LIGHT LEVELS

OUTSIDE   INSIDE

Full sun.
Dappled shade in hottest months.

TEMPERATURE RANGE

°F -10 0 10 20 30 40 50 60 70 80 90 100

Hardy species: tolerates freezing for brief periods. Place in unheated greenhouse in severe weather. Tender species: minimum 41°F, ideally maintain between 54–68°F.

PESTS AND DISEASES

Aphids, scale insects. Spider mites may invade congested plants. Fireblight appears as black patches on the flowers, and causes dieback, eventually killing the tree. Best policy is to burn the tree as soon as fireblight is diagnosed, to stop infection spreading.

SOIL

ORGANIC 60%	GRIT 40%

Repot every year at first; later every two years.

WATERING

SPRING	SUMMER	FALL	WINTER
🌢🌢🌢	🌢 🌢🌢	🌢🌢	🌢🌢

Keep the plant moist at all times. Drought will cause dieback and retard flowering.

FEEDING

SPRING	SUMMER	FALL	WINTER
🌢	🌢	🌢	

Balanced fertilizer throughout growing season. Low-nitrogen feed in fall.

PRUNING

Prune extension growth in fall. Cut other branches back to selected flowering spurs in spring.

RHODODENDRON INDICUM

Satsuki azalea

HARDY

Satsuki azaleas come in all shapes, sizes, and colors. This semi-specimen has a good trunk and branch structure which will develop into a fine specimen with careful attention.

and delicacy of form are far superior. They might be considered disproportionately large for the tree, but this is satsuki, and the normal rules don't apply to the strict satsuki enthusiast. Having said that, many large specimen satsuki bonsai are mighty fine trees in their own right, and are more often than not exhibited for their heavy, tapered trunks and fine neat foliage, without a flower to be seen. It is true to say that the flowers do distract from the authentic tree-like image, but once seen, they become irresistible.

All azaleas have three major horticultural requirements.

• They need a constantly moist soil. They will not tolerate dry roots.

• They require a lime-free soil. Use peat or ericaceous compost and lime-free grit. If you live in a hard water area (where the domestic water supply contains calcium), use rainwater.

• They prefer dappled or partial shade to imitate their natural woodland margin habitat.

Growth can be vigorous, particularly after pruning. The long, slender red shoots, which can grow ⅔ of an inch in a day, quickly become brittle, so wire training must be carried out before midsummer.

Maintenance pruning is a simple routine. Immediately after

IN JAPAN, SATSUKI azaleas fall into a class of their own. There are bonsai, and there are satsuki bonsai.

Unlike spring-flowering garden azaleas, the satsuki flowers in midsummer, at the terminals of short current shoots. The range of flower color and pattern is bewildering, and

the selective hybridization adds to it each year. Some of the most valued varieties, such as "Eikan" can have white, pink and bicolored flowers on the same branch at the same time.

Satsuki flowers are large compared with those of garden azaleas, but the intensity of color

flowering, cut out all new shoots. Further new shoots are just lightly trimmed to shape as necessary during the summer. Pruning branches in summer encourages growth, pruning in fall is less likely to. It is important for plant hygiene to remove all dead or damaged flowers without delay.

Although this azalea has had little training, it has a good, sturdy trunk and, if the flower color satisfies you, it is worth buying.

What to look for

Azalea trunks thicken and taper easily, so you should not accept one that does not. Although branches can be grown from scratch if necessary, there is no reason why you shouldn't be able to find an example that already has a good basic branch framework. Don't rely on the label to tell you the color; it will only give you a rough idea. It makes more sense to buy your satsuki in early to midsummer, when you can spend hours trying to make up your mind which color to buy.

Points to watch

Lime in the soil or water will damage the tree by "locking" the nutrients and rendering them inaccessible to the plant. The leaves turn yellow, growth slows, and eventually the tree dies. Some fertilizers are also slightly alkaline, so restrict your choice to those recommended for ericaceous plants or calcifuges.

RHODODENDRON INDICUM

BONSAI SOURCES

Japan.

LIGHT LEVELS

OUTSIDE   INSIDE

Semi-shade.

TEMPERATURE RANGE

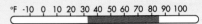

°F -10 0 10 20 30 40 50 60 70 80 90 100

Azaleas become tired in hot climates. A summer maximum of 86°F and winter minimum of 32°F is best. Avoid heavy frosts by placing in an unheated garage or shed. Do not bring indoors in winter.

PESTS AND DISEASES

Aphids and scale insects. Vine weevils may chew notches in the leaves, but their larvae are more dangerous to the roots. If you see evidence of adults feeding on leaves, treat your entire collection with parasitic nematodes immediately.

SOIL

ORGANIC 70%	GRIT 30%

Use only acid or lime-free ingredients. Adding some chopped sphagnum moss to the soil helps keep the plant happy. Repot every two to three years, immediately after flowering.

WATERING

SPRING	SUMMER	FALL	WINTER

Use lime-free water. Water frequently in growing season and maintain moistness in winter. Never allow soil to dry out.

FEEDING

SPRING	SUMMER	FALL	WINTER

Gentle balanced feed until flowering begins, low-nitrogen from end of flowering until fall. Check that fertilizer is suitable for ericaceous or calcifuge plants.

PRUNING

Cut back all new shoots immediately after flowering. Lightly trim further growth to shape.

SAGERETIA THEEZANS

Sageretia

TENDER

NATIVE TO SOUTHERN China, this evergreen shrub is now used for commercial bonsai production throughout the subtropical regions of Asia. It is one of the most popular species used for indoor bonsai in temperate regions.

The trunk and thick branches appear to be as hard as iron. The smooth bark is relatively thin and regularly sheds large gray-buff flakes, leaving brighter, almost orange patches in an ever-changing pattern. The growth is angular, so trunks are either full of sharp bends or ramrod straight with thinner angular branches growing from the top, depending on the original nursery.

When heavy roots have been exposed to the air for a few years they, too, begin to shed patches and appear every bit as old and full of character as the trunk. This is used to full advantage, and the vast majority of *Sageretia* bonsai display grotesque, dramatic, exposed roots. In China, *Sageretia* bonsai, whose roots and trunks look like animals, birds or dragons, are particularly sought after.

The bright, shiny leaves are small and are borne at very short intervals on slender shoots. These shoots are surprisingly brittle when young, but become more pliable after a few months. Shoots and leaves are so prolific that there is no need to employ subtle trimming techniques. Once the branch lines are established, you simply clip the foliage to shape – just like trimming a hedge. Keep the trunk and main branch line free of stray shoots

Clean trunks and branch lines, as well as neatly clipped foliage. An object lesson in bonsai refinement.

The dramatic twin trunks of this *Sageretia* are reminiscent of two dragons playing. The Chinese adore bonsai that are evocative of such images. The bark regularly flakes, leaving an ever-changing patchwork.

which will obscure the view of the inner parts of the tree. Branches can be reshaped, or foliage clouds divided by harder pruning. Very little wiring should be necessary.

Constant clipping of this nature inevitably induces more shoots to grow than could possibly survive such congestion. Periodically, clean out all the dead twigs and snags from the inner foliage cloud. Standing the tree on a high table and approaching it from below not only makes access easier, but it is the best way to analyze the branch formation of any bonsai. After all, that is one of the angles we view all trees from, isn't it?

Being accustomed to the shade of taller trees in the subtropics, *Sageretia* likes a humid atmosphere and dislikes too much hot sun.

What to look for

The most important consideration is the trunk line. They will all be totally different, so choose one that suits your taste. Branch areas can be built up very quickly. Check the plant all around, not just at the front. When stored close together, *Sageretia* often lose entire branches. Any areas of foliage that appear to be dying, probably are, so leave that tree on the shelf.

Points to watch

Sageretia are easy to keep, indoors or out, provided they are given sufficient heat and humidity. Cold damp weather or a hot dry atmosphere are equally likely to cause loss of foliage and dieback of young shoots.

SAGERETIA THEEZANS

BONSAI SOURCES

China. Korea, Taiwan and other sources developing.

LIGHT LEVELS

OUTSIDE   INSIDE

Partial shade.

TEMPERATURE RANGE

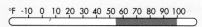

°F -10 0 10 20 30 40 50 60 70 80 90 100

Minimum 54°F in winter. At this temperature, foliage loss may occur. Growth will continue in temperatures of 64°F and above.

PESTS AND DISEASES

 Aphids and red spider mites enjoy young shoots in crowded foliage. Spray regularly as a precaution. Yellowing foliage and lack of vigor could be caused by mineral deficiency. Sprinkle soil with trace elements and apply sequestered iron.

SOIL

ORGANIC	GRIT
40%	**60%**

Repot every two to three years. A deep pot can conserve moisture and create localized humidity.

WATERING

SPRING	SUMMER	FALL	WINTER
💧💧💧	💧💧💧	💧💧💧	💧💧

Water lavishly when in full growth. Keep the soil well moistened in winter. Spray foliage with tepid water at least once a day.

FEEDING

SPRING	SUMMER	FALL	WINTER
💧	💧	💧	

Balanced feed when in growth. Stop feeding when tree stops growing and recommence two weeks after growth starts.

PRUNING

Any time of year. When trimming, take care not to cut through individual leaves.

SERISSA FOETIDA

Tree of a thousand stars

TENDER

THE BOTANICAL AND common names of this native of China indicate its dual personality. The small white flowers which can appear in flushes throughout the year, have five narrow petals and contrast with the sombre, dark green, shiny leaves. When seen at dusk, the reason for such a romantic common name is obvious. On the other hand, *foetida* comes from the Latin word for bad smell, and refers to the unpleasant odor of the damp trunk and roots in the boggy ground. Don't panic – this is hardly noticeable on a bonsai. But the warm humid atmosphere of subtropical Asia is a different story!

In nature, *Serissa* is a sprawling, bushy plant that seldom has a discernible trunk. It is also difficult to create a good strong trunk in bonsai, so they tend to follow multi-trunked or low, spreading styles. Frequently, the growers will increase the apparent trunk height by exposing considerable lengths of root which are squeezed close together. In time, these roots will fuse together to form a strong trunk base, but it takes many years of healthy growth for this to happen. For this reason, specimen serissas are rare and expensive.

Smaller commercial trees can become specimens in time. This process can be speeded up by planting the tree in a much larger

container and allowing it to grow unhindered for a few years. Regular feeding and good growing conditions are essential. After two or three years, you will be amazed at how the trunk and exposed roots have matured. The branches will, of course, be dreadfully overgrown, but they can be cut right back to the trunk if necessary, and they can be

quickly rebuilt while the tree is still in the large container. When you are happy with the shape, you can replant the bonsai in a more suitable pot at the next appropriate time.

The leaves are borne at very short intervals on the shoots, so you can just clip the foliage clouds to shape as necessary. Avoid cutting through individual leaves as they will discolor and spoil the tree. Cutting each shoot individually is a good discipline and an excellent way to familiarize yourself with your tree. Old crowded twigs can be pruned out at any time, to allow air and light into the structure.

What to look for

Specimens are rare, but you can still look for a potential specimen. Try to imagine what the tree could look like in years to come. If you don't want to go to the trouble of developing your own bonsai, choose one of the multi-trunked or group plantings, which require less dominant trunks.

Points to watch

Serissa like humidity and wet roots. However, the flowers deteriorate if they do not dry quickly enough after spraying. Ensure good air circulation at all times and spray less often when in flower.

No wonder this plant is called "tree of a thousand stars." Masses of tiny, white, star-shaped flowers can appear at any time of year.

Almost all commercial *Serissa* are planted in too shallow pots with too many unnecessary rocks and ornaments. Nevertheless, if the plant looks like a tree, it is worth buying – you can always throw the junk away!

SERISSA FOETIDA

BONSAI SOURCES

China at first; now also other Asian sources.

LIGHT LEVELS

OUTSIDE   INSIDE

Full sun.
Shade pot if near a sunny window.

TEMPERATURE RANGE

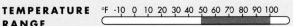
°F -10 0 10 20 30 40 50 60 70 80 90 100

Minimum winter temperature 50°F. Some foliage loss may occur at this temperature. Ideally maintain around 68°F.

PESTS AND DISEASES

Aphids, scale insects and spider mites. Spray regularly as a precaution. Powdery mildew is troublesome on trees grown in poorly ventilated rooms.

SOIL

ORGANIC 80%	GRIT 20%

Repot every two years in early spring. Hold your nose!

WATERING

SPRING	SUMMER	FALL	WINTER

 Serissa is very thirsty. Water as normal, but never allow to become even slightly dry. Stand in a tray of water to ensure constantly wet soil while in full growth. In winter, remove from the tray, but keep moist. Spray regularly, but don't drench flowers.

FEEDING

SPRING	SUMMER	FALL	WINTER

 Balanced fertilizer when in growth. Weak low-nitrogen feed if growing slowly in winter. No feed if growth has stopped.

PRUNING

Any time. Cut shoots back to maintain shape, and thin crowded areas as necessary.

STEWARTIA MONADELPHA

Stewartia/Stuartia

HARDY

THIS IS A dwarf form of the small, native Japanese tree, also sometimes known as "deciduous camellia." The large open white flowers are reason enough to make this species desirable, and so is the spectacular fall foliage. But it is the gorgeous smooth, orange bark that is its outstanding feature.

In spite of the flowers, stewartias are treasured for their winter image. As the bark ages, it becomes almost purple and flakes off in large patches to reveal a new orange layer beneath. This constantly changing pattern is fascinating, but for display purposes all old bark is flaked off. The fresh orange bark is so smooth it appears to be polished. However, it is soft, and easily damaged while wiring.

The shoots naturally grow strongly upwards. Rather than fight against this habit, the bonsai artist uses it to produce a tree whose branches sweep gracefully outwards and upwards from the trunk. Secondary branches and twigs follow the same pattern. Little wiring is necessary, since the branch shapes can be created by pruning alone. Buds stand vertically like little green candles, at the tips and sides of the twigs. When caught by the sun, the rhythm of the branches, twigs and buds, combined with the color of the bark, produces an awe-inspiring

The upward sweep of the branches on this specimen of stewartia, coupled with the pale green leaves, create an enchanting image as the buds open in spring.

image that seems to flicker and dance like a flame against the pale blue winter sky.

Stewartias are lime-haters. They must be planted in acid soil, so check ingredients for alkalinity. To be safe, use a brand ericaceous compost for the organic content. You should also use rainwater, and lots of it, unless you live in an area where the domestic water supply is totally lime-free. Stewartias are thirsty and do not tolerate even partial drying of

The smooth orange bark of stewartia is unique among deciduous bonsai species, and is its main attraction to bonsai collectors.

"Starter" trees like this are relatively expensive in comparison to most other species. Nevertheless, the cost is justified by the potentially beautiful image that can result after a few years' careful training.

the soil – their leaves are thin and will wilt and shrivel at the slightest provocation. Wind and hot sun will also cause leaves to scorch or fall, so position your bonsai where it will receive no direct sun after mid-morning, and is sheltered from wind. The shade of a house is better than an overhead tree as it allows unrestricted overhead light.

What to look for
Pruning scars heal very quickly on stewartia, and if they are properly hollowed and sealed, they will disappear and become completely smooth. If badly executed, the healing bark will form an unsightly lump which spoils the smooth bark. If buying a tree in leaf, take extra trouble to examine the hidden trunk and branches, and imagine how they would appear in winter. A good surface root formation is also an important consideration.

Points to watch
Stewartias are not easy to keep. It may take you a year or two to get the soil, watering and feeding right, but when you do, the reward will be worth the effort.

STEWARTIA MONADELPHA

BONSAI SOURCES
Japan.

LIGHT LEVELS

Partial shade; full sun in fall improves color.

TEMPERATURE RANGE

Give additional shade and spray foliage in really hot weather. Withstands frost well, but should be protected from prolonged freezing by being placed in a garage or shed.

PESTS AND DISEASES

Occasional aphids and caterpillars.

SOIL

ORGANIC 80%	GRIT 20%

Use only guaranteed lime-free ingredients. Repot every two to three years. Cut thick roots back hard; cut less from fine roots.

WATERING

Use only rainwater or guaranteed lime-free water from the faucet. Water lavishly in summer. Do not stand the pot in a water tray as this will waterlog the soil, but never allow soil to become dry. Reduce water slightly in winter.

FEEDING

Use only fertilizers recommended for heathers, camellias and other lime-haters. Balanced feed in summer and nitrogen-free from late summer onwards.

PRUNING
Cut back all shoots regularly to two or three leaves. Cut above a bud which faces outwards. Prune out shoots that spoil the regular pattern of branches. Keep the design open.

TAXUS CUSPIDATA

Japanese yew

HARDY

JAPANESE YEW IS very similar to the European *Taxus baccata*, the major differences being that its leaves have paler undersides, and its bark retains its juvenile yellow-gray color for longer, before becoming dark chestnut-brown. In practice, the two species are identical in their requirements and treatment.

Yews are slow growers, so inexpensive trees are rare and often of very poor quality. Specimen trees are sometimes exported from Japan, and these are normally superb quality *yamadori* (collected from the wild). They are naturally expensive, but nevertheless good value if you can afford it. Some large Western bonsai producers have begun to distribute medium-priced yew bonsai to retail outlets. These tend to be better value.

Branches are very flexible and springy. Copper wire is best for yews as it is stronger than aluminum. It will have to be cut off and replaced at least once before the branch has set in position. Even after a branch has apparently set, it will gradually creep upwards over a month or so. Use fine wire ties to pull branches down – attach the other end to the pot or a heavy exposed root. Young side shoots will set rigidly in a relatively short time if they are wired when a year old and then allowed to grow vigorously.

Yews like to be pruned back hard. They respond with a fresh crop of crowded new shoots which can be thinned and trained. Long, bare branches can be rejuvenated by cutting them back to about half in early summer, causing strong replacement shoots.

Extension shoots are round with the leaves growing in a spiral. Side shoots are flatter and finer, with the leaves carried only at the sides.

On established trees, extension shoots should be cut out completely. If you want to use them, wire them when they are young. Side shoots should merely be trimmed to shape. Any that grow straight up or hang below the branch line are trimmed off. Those growing sideways are shortened by one- to two-thirds. This regime will gradually build a wide, low-domed cloud of foliage on each branch.

Yews do not like persistent sun. Bonsai should be in at least dappled shade all the year round.

The old driftwood on the trunk has aged and weathered beautifully and accentuated the natural grain. The harsh white of the lime sulphur has mellowed to a silvery-gray.

The rich green, mature needles of Japanese yew are highlighted by the fresher spring growth. The neat, dense foliage is in perfect proportion to the tree.

What to look for

Unless you are wealthy, don't look for specimen yew. Set your sights on what is in reality a semi-trained bonsai. It should have an interesting clear trunkline and spreading surface roots. Look for a tree with well-spaced branches sweeping downwards from the trunk.

Points to watch

Beware: the foliage and fruit of both species are extremely poisonous. Yews are very hardy, and can take severe cold, but they are also moisture lovers. If their roots are frozen solid, they cannot replace moisture loss through wind or winter sun. Yew should be kept shaded and sheltered from wind all year.

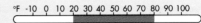

TAXUS CUSPIDATA

BONSAI SOURCES

Japan; home-produced bonsai now available.

LIGHT LEVELS

OUTSIDE INSIDE

Partial or full shade.

TEMPERATURE RANGE

°F -10 0 10 20 30 40 50 60 70 80 90 100

Dislikes hot summers with temperatures constantly over 90°F. Needs cold winters and tolerates freezing well. Do not allow to remain frozen solid for more than a week at a time. Do not bring indoors in the winter.

PESTS AND DISEASES

Scale insects and spider mites.

SOIL

ORGANIC 70%	GRIT 30%

Use larger-than-usual particles of organic matter to maintain water retention but to increase drainage. Repot every three years. Use a deepish pot.

WATERING

SPRING	SUMMER	FALL	WINTER

Keep well moistened in summer. Even moisture is better than "drenching-and-drying," and is easy to achieve in the shade. Minimum watering in winter. Shelter from prolonged rain.

FEEDING

SPRING	SUMMER	FALL	WINTER

Weak balanced feed all summer. Low-nitrogen top-up in early fall.

PRUNING

Prune at any time. Cut out vigorous shoots and shorten all others. Clean dangling shoots.

ULMUS PARVIFOLIA

Chinese elm

HARDY

THIS IS WITHOUT question the best elm for bonsai training, and has been used to create famous masterpieces as well as countless thousands of commercial bonsai of all sizes and prices throughout its native China, Korea and Japan. In its natural state, *Ulmus parvifolia* is a small tree which is used for hedging purposes because of its readiness to produce masses of new shoots after it has been pruned.

There are several forms of Chinese elm – some with thick, corky bark, others with less attractive smooth gray bark, but all have similar growth habits. The leaves are small, glossy green, with serrated edges, and are borne densely on fine shoots. Bonsai originating from Japan are hardy, and can be frozen for short periods. However, the fleshy roots may disintegrate if the soil is frozen solid while saturated.

Commercial bonsai originating from China are often grown in the root-over-rock style, which produces a powerful base that compensates for the somewhat slender trunk.

When kept outdoors in a temperate climate, they will shed its leaves in fall. When kept indoors, the leaves will remain green until spring, when they will fall as new growth begins.

Bonsai from China and Korea are sometimes wrongly named as *Zelkova sinica*, possibly to circumvent import restrictions. Although hardy, they are not accustomed to freezing conditions, and are intended to be kept indoors in temperate climates. They are perfectly happy outside all winter if the temperatures rarely reach freezing, but expect some loss of foliage.

In fact, loss of foliage is the Chinese elm's way of responding to trauma of any kind. Moving the tree from one room to another, sudden changes in temperature, drought, waterlogging, and systemic chemical sprays can all cause sudden defoliation. However, it is soon replaced and the tree continues as if nothing had happened.

Trimming is easy. Once the general framework of the tree is established, you cut each new shoot back to two leaves as soon as it grows out of line. This will inevitably result in two new shoots. This doubling of shoots three or four times a year quickly builds up masses of

A smaller tree than the one opposite, but with a trunk that is more in proportion to its overall size. Selective branch pruning and regular clipping will eventually produce a fine specimen.

dense twigs. Every winter, prune out dead areas or branch tips which have become too heavy.

What to look for

Chinese elm is one of the few species that can recreate almost a perfect little tree – corky bark, fine tracery of twigs, etc. Look for a bonsai that has natural looking root flare, trunk line and basic branch placement. Long, wayward branches don't matter; these can be cut back or removed, but the basic frame must be tree-like from the beginning.

Points to watch

Systemic insecticides and fungicides cause defoliation in Chinese elms. The roots are fleshy and contain a lot of water. If the balance between the water in the roots and that in the soil is disturbed – rapid drying or heavy rain – and the pot is then frozen, the roots will "explode" or "implode" when the water expands as it freezes.

ULMUS PARVIFOLIA

BONSAI SOURCES

Japan, China, Korea.

LIGHT LEVELS

OUTSIDE   INSIDE

Full sun.
Small pots need shading to prevent drying out. Do not expose to direct sun through a window.

TEMPERATURE RANGE

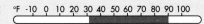
°F -10 0 10 20 30 40 50 60 70 80 90 100

Can withstand light frost, but best protected from freezing. A minimum of 45–50°F will prevent total leaf fall.

PESTS AND DISEASES

Aphids, scale insects, occasional spider mites indoors. Mildew if air circulation is poor and roots are dry. Do not use systemics on elms.

SOIL

ORGANIC 60%	GRIT 40%

Repot every year or two.

WATERING

SPRING	SUMMER	FALL	WINTER

Water well in summer; maintain evenly moist in winter. Water less if leaves fall.

FEEDING

SPRING	SUMMER	FALL	WINTER

Balanced feed until the late summer. Nitrogen-free from then until leaf fall. If the plant is kept indoors, continue with a half-strength balanced feed all winter.

PRUNING

Prune at any time indoors, in mid-spring outdoors, just before buds burst. Trim to two leaves per shoot in summer.

WISTERIA

Wisteria

HARDY

IN EARLY SUMMER, when wisteria are in full flower, they are the most spectacular of all garden climbers. The long racemes of purple or mauve flowers are borne in such profusion that they completely conceal the wall or fence. The foliage at this stage is only beginning to emerge.

As a bonsai, too, it is a breathtaking sight in flower. Unfortunately, when the flowers have gone, and it starts to grow, your wisteria will quickly become a rampant mess. Being a climber, long, twining shoots with large compound leaves will spring out in search of support, growing at a phenomenal rate. Naturally, these must be kept under control.

Let the shoots grow until they begin to invade neighboring trees, then prune them back to two or three leaves. Repeat this after a few weeks when more shoots have grown. You may need to prune four or five times during the growing season. Next year, when flowering is over, prune out about half the congested stubs and spurs from last year's battle, leaving those facing upwards or outwards.

Sometimes an individual wisteria seems reluctant to flower. It may be that it was grown from seed, and is not yet old enough to flower, but this is unlikely – most wisteria are grown from cuttings. A diet of low-nitrogen fertilizer, applied at the

A rare specimen wisteria that has been developed from an ancient plant collected from open ground. The heavy, hollow trunk indicates this bonsai's great age. You can see from the size of the flowers that the tree measures almost 3 ft in width.

maximum rate recommended by the manufacturer, might bring results. But the cause is more likely to be cultural. Wisteria, like all climbers, are designed to have their roots in the cool, moist soil at the base of taller structures, while their foliage and flowers are exposed to the full sun. To imitate this, use a deep pot and keep the base shaded, but allow the leaves full sun. Stand the pot in a shallow dish of water that can be drawn up into the pot through the drainage holes. The water should be deep enough to last all day.

There is only one style suitable for wisteria. When in flower, the racemes cascade like the tresses of a weeping willow, and this is the style to follow. Don't try to style your wisteria like a tree when in leaf; it is not practical. Concentrate on those wonderful flowers.

What to look for

Being climbers, the trunks are seldom very thick unless they are collected from the wild. They generally have interesting shapes and curves, with heavily pruned spurs at the top, on which you will build. Choose a tree with a tall trunk with rhythmic curves and, if possible, a strong-looking surface root formation.

Points to watch

Hot dry roots are debilitating to wisterias. Roots shrivel and die, sometimes killing parts of the tree. Pruning shoots too soon will retard flowering. Delay until it really becomes essential, then prune hard.

LEFT
This grafted offering has a good sturdy trunk and well-placed branches – ideal for further development. What's more, it clearly loves to flower.

WISTERIA

BONSAI SOURCES

China, Japan.

LIGHT LEVELS

OUTSIDE   INSIDE

Full sun on foliage; shade pots. Not suitable for indoors.

TEMPERATURE RANGE

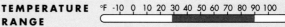

°F -10 0 10 20 30 40 50 60 70 80 90 100

Tolerates freezing – protect from prolonged severe freezing by placing in a garage or shed. Do not saturate soil with water in freezing weather.

PESTS AND DISEASES

Aphids, scale insects. Bud-drop may occur if soil is too dry. Chlorosis (yellowing leaves) may occur if soil is too alkaline. Apply a brand soil acidifier.

SOIL

ORGANIC	GRIT
60%	40%

Repot every three years unless it becomes potbound before then. Use a deep pot.

WATERING

SPRING	SUMMER	FALL	WINTER
🌢🌢🌢	🌢🌢🌢	🌢🌢🌢	🌢🌢

Water lavishly in growing season. Pot can be stood in water in summer. Keep well moistened, but not saturated in winter.

FEEDING

SPRING	SUMMER	FALL	WINTER
	🌢	🌢	

Regular low-nitrogen feed from the end of flowering right through to fall. Finish with a nitrogen-free feed before leaf fall.

PRUNING

Prune out congested areas after flowering. Prune all long shoots back to a few leaves as necessary.

ZELKOVA SERRATA

Japanese gray-bark elm

HARDY

ALONG WITH BLACK pine, zelkovas are one of the most commonly planted park and street trees in Japan. In nature, it has the stereotypical tree shape with branches fanning out from the top of a straight, clean trunk. The branches divide and become thinner at regular intervals, terminating in a tracery of fine, outward pointing twigs, and forming an even dome-shaped silhouette.

In classical bonsai, this is repeated exactly in miniature, and is known as the broom style – *hokidachi* in Japanese. Some specimens are almost a yard tall, while others are small enough to stand on the palm of your hand. The process is not difficult, but it takes time, so commercial growers offer semi-trained bonsai which have had the basic work done, but need refining and further development.

In small bonsai, limit the number of branches coming from the top of the trunk to three. In larger trees, you can allow five. In summer, prune each branch back so that the remaining portion is about a third the length of the trunk. New shoots will emerge from around the wound. Select two or three strong shoots and cut them back to two leaves. Remove the rest. From now on, allow all new shoots to grow to four or five leaves and then cut

A clean, straight trunk is essential for the classic "broom" style in which zelkovas are almost invariably trained.

them back to two; remove over-crowded ones completely. Repeat this process for the life of the bonsai. Every few years, prune hard back to old wood, to regenerate the tree and to keep it in proportion.

Young zelkovas whose trunks are not straight enough for the broom style are often planted in groups. These can vary from five trees up to twenty-five or more. When grown in this way, the fine twigs create very realistic effects, especially in winter. Because zelkovas are generally propagated from seed, they are all slightly different. Some will leaf out before others in spring, some will have leaves with a reddish tint at the edges, others are bright green. Some will turn yellow in fall, some orange. A large forest of zelkovas, showing all these colour variations, is full of interest and captivates the viewer in all seasons.

What to look for

When buying a broom style, look first for a spreading, evenly distributed pattern of surface roots. Next, look for a straight trunk with branches emerging from the same point at the top. They should emerge smoothly, not at a sharp angle, and should sit centrally on top of the trunk, not to one side.

When choosing a group, ensure that all the trees are healthy. Any that are unstable and rock easily have poor roots. The trunks should vary in thickness and height, with the tallest ones towards the center of the composition. If you're not entirely happy with the arrangement, you can alter it when repotting.

Points to watch

Because zelkovas produce so many shoots, they can become congested. The fine twigs, starved of light and air, will die back. As often as not, if an area becomes too congested, it will all die, not just the weakest shoots. Sometimes, whole branches can be lost. It is important to keep the structure light and airy.

Specimen zelkovas vary in size from a few inches to 3 feet tall. This medium-sized specimen is very tree-like in appearance and is developing well.

ZELKOVA SERRATA

BONSAI SOURCES

Japan.

LIGHT LEVELS

OUTSIDE INSIDE

Full sun.
Protect from afternoon sun in really hot weather.

TEMPERATURE RANGE

°F -10 0 10 20 30 40 50 60 70 80 90 100

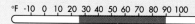

Shade if temperature exceeds 86°F. Roots tolerate freezing, but fine twigs may die back if exposed to cold winds.

PESTS AND DISEASES

Aphids, scale insects, occasional caterpillars.

SOIL

ORGANIC 60%	GRIT 40%

Repot every year, older trees every two to three years.

WATERING

SPRING	SUMMER	FALL	WINTER
🌢🌢🌢	🌢🌢🌢	🌢🌢	🌢

Keep moist at all times.

FEEDING

SPRING	SUMMER	FALL	WINTER
🌢	🌢	🌢	

Balanced feed from late spring to the end of summer, nitrogen-free from then until leaf-fall.

PRUNING

Prune for growth in summer. Remove unwanted branches in early spring. Trim to two leaves as necessary.

SUPPLIERS AND USEFUL ADDRESSES

MAGAZINES

Bonsai
Bonsai Clubs International
2636 W. Mission Road #277
Tallahassee, FL 32304
904/575-1442

Bonsai Today
Stone Lantern Publishing Co.
PO Box 816
Sudbury, MA 01776
508/443-7110
Books available

International Bonsai
International Bonsai Arboretum
PO Box 23894
Rochester, NY 14692-3894
716/334-2595

BONSAI SUPPLIERS

The following offer a mail order service for tools and equipment; many will also supply trees by mail.

Bennett's Bonsai Nursery
1816 Farfax Ave
Metairie, LA 70003
504/888-7994

Bonsai Arts
113 East 8680 South
Sandy, UT 84070
801/278-9555

Bonsai Center
101 N. Groesbeck, Suite B
Mt. Clemens, MI 48083
810/465-955

Bonsai Farm
Rt. 1, Box 130
LaVernia, TX 78121
210/649-2109

Bonsai Farm
13827 Highway 875
Adkins, TX 78101
210/649-2109

Bonsai by the Monastery
2625 Highway 212 SW Box T
Conyers, GA 30208
404/918-9661

Bonsai Nursery Inc.
3750 S. Federal Blvd.
Englewood, CO 80110
303/761-3066

Bonsai Showcase
2 Stuart Street
Hudson, NH 03051
605/882-8252

Bonsai West
100 Great Road
PO Box 1291
Littlejohn, MA 01460
508/486-3556

Brussel's Bonsai Nursery
8365 Center Hill Road
Olive Branch, MS 38654
800/582-2593

D & B Bonsai Co.
289 Clementon Road
Berlin, NJ 08009
609/783-4212

DuPont Bonsai
PO Box 375
Newberg, OR 97132-0375
503/538-6071

International Bonsai Arboretum
PO Box 23894
Rochester, NY 14692-3894
716/334-2595

Jiu-San Bonsai
1243 Melville Road
Farmingdale, NY 11535
516/293-9246

Lone Tree Bonsai
5998 Rt 96
Farmington, NY 14425
716/742-8550

Maine Bonsai Gardens
RR#3 Box 502
Wiscasset, ME 04578
207/882-7901

Matsu Momiji Nursery
205 Quick Road
Elkview, WV 25071
304/965-2705

Miami Tropical Bonsai
14775 SW232nd Street
Homestead, FL 33170
305/258-0865

Minnesota Bonsai Society
4640 Wild Canyon Drive
Woodbury, MN 55125
612/459-7162

New England Bonsai Gardens, Inc.
914 South Main Street (Rt126)
Bellingham, MA 02019-1846
800/457-5445

Oriental Garden
307 Disbrow Hill Road
Perrineville, NJ 08535
609/490-0705

Plant City Bonsai
5607 Cleveland Highway (129 N)
Clermont, GA 30527
770/535-2991

Re-Sieg Bonsai Company
7711 South Street
Lincoln, NE 68506

Riverside Bonsai
PO Box 633
Columbus, NC 28722
704/894-3735

Rosade Bonsai Studio
6912 Ely Road
New Hope, PA 18938
215/862-5925

Shanti Bithi Nursery
3047 High Ridge Road
Stamford, CT 06903
203/329-0768

Wildwood Gardens
14488 Rock Creek Road
Chardon, OH 44024
216/286-3714

BONSAI ORGANIZATIONS

The following national organizations will be able to direct you to your local bonsai club, or help you set up your own.

The American Bonsai Society
PO Box 1136
Puyallup, WA 98371-1136

Bonsai Clubs International
2636 W. Mission Road #277
Tallahassee, FL 32304
904/575-1442

INDEX

Page numbers in *italics* refer to illustrations.

A

Acer (maple) 6, *16-17*
  buergerianum (trident maple) *11*, *12-13*, 58-9, *58-9*
  palmatum (Japanese maple):
    'Chishio' 62-3, *62-3*
    'Deshojo' 62-3, *62-3*
    'Kiyohime' 64-5, *64-5*
    'Seigen' 66-7, *66-7*
adelgids 55, *55*
air quality 25-6
ants 53
aphids 51, *51*, 53, *53*, 55, 61
apples 44
apricot, Japanese flowering *39*, 134-5, *134-5*
Arundinaria 68-9
azalea 44, 142-3, *142*, *143*

B

bamboos 68-9, *68-9*
  sacred 118-19, *118-19*
beech, *see Fagus crenata*
black spot 51, *51*
Bougainvillea 70-1, *70-1*
branch structure 17-18, *16*, *17*, *18*
broadleaved trees 42, *43*
buying bonsai 14-19

C

care 21-31
Carmona microphylla 14, 72-3, *72-3*
Carpinus (hornbeam) *74-5*
  laxiflora 74-5
  turczaninowii 74-5
cedar, Japanese 86-7, *86-7*
Celtis sinensis 76-7, *76-7*
Chaenomeles 78-9, *78-9*
  speciosa 78
Chamaecyparis obtusa 80-1, *80-1*
chemicals 50
cherries 44
Chinese bonsai 8
  classical *11*
collections 9, *9-10*
conifers:
  leaf pruning *40-1*
  regeneration pruning 42, *42*
Cotoneaster 82-3, *82-3*
  horizontalis 82
  microphyllus 82

Crab apple 112-13, *112-13*
Crape myrtle 108-9, *108-9*
Crassula 84-5, *84-5*
  arborescens 84
Cryptomeria japonica 86-7, *86-7*
  j. yatsubusa 86
Cycas (cycad) *15*, 88-9, *88-9*
  circinnalis 88
  revoluta 88
cypress, hinoki 80-1, *80-1*

D

diseases 49-55, 57
displaying bonsai 23-5, *22-5*, 26
dried-out trees, saving *28-9*

E

Ehretia buxifolia, see Carmona microphylla
elm *18*
  Chinese 152-3, *152*, *153*
  Japanese gray-bark 156-7, *156-7*
environment 22-7

F

Fagus crenata 90-1, *90-1*
feeding 30-1, 57
fertilizers 30-1
Ficus (fig) *20-1*, 92-3, *92-3*
  benjamina 92
  microphylla 92
  retusa 92
firethorn, *see Pyracantha*
foliage, *see* leaves
Fuchsia 94-5, *94-5*
  microphylla 94
Fukien tea 14, 72-3, *72-3*
fungal diseases 26, 49-55
fungi 55

G

gall mites 55
Ginkgo biloba 96-7, *96-7*

H

hackberry, Chinese 76-7, *76-7*
half-hardy plants 15
hardiness 56
hardy plants 15
Hinoki cypress 80-1, *80-1*
history 8-10
holly, Japanese 98-9, *98*, *99*
hornbeam, *see Carpinus*
humidity 25
hygiene 50

I

Ilex crenata 98-9, *98*, *99*
insecticides 50

J

Jade tree 84-5, *84-5*
Japanese bonsai 9-10
  classical *11*
Jasmine orange, 114-15, *114-15*
Jasminum nudiflorum 100-1, *100-1*
Juniperus (juniper):
  chinensis, sargentii 102-3, *102-3*
  leaf pruning *41*
  regeneration pruning 42, *42*
  rigida 104-5, *104-5*
  squamata, 'Meyeri' 106-7, *106-7*
  wiring 46, *47*

L

Lagerstroemia indica 108-9, *108-9*
landscape, miniature 8, *8*
leaf miners 52, *52*
leaf pruning *40-1*
leaves:
  discolored 51, *51*, 50
  distorted 53, *53*
  dry 52, 54
  ragged 54
  spraying 25
  wilted 52-3
light 22-4, 57
Ligustrum (privet) *15*, 19
  sinense (Chinese) 110-11, *110*, *111*

M

maidenhair tree, 96-7, *96-7*
Malus 112-13, *112-13*
  cerasifera 112
  halliana 112
maple, *see Acer*
money tree 84-5, *84-5*
Murraya paniculata 114-15, *114-15*
myrtle, crape 108-9, *108-9*
Myrtus (myrtle) 116-17, *116-17*

N

Nandica domestica 118-19, *118-19*
nematodes, parasitic 53, *53*
nutrients 30-1

O

Olea (olive) *15*
  europaea 120-1, *120*, *121*
Omiya 10, *10-11*

P

peach leaf curl 53, *53*
Peking, Imperial Gardens 8
pests 49-55, 57
photosynthesis 22
Picea (spruce) 122-3, *122-3*
  abies 'Little Gem' 122
  glehnii 122
  mariana 'Nana' 122
Pinus (pine) 14
  densiflora 124-5, *125-6*
  leaf pruning 40
  parviflora (*P. pentaphylla*) 126-7, *126-7*
  pests 55
  regeneration pruning 42, *42*
  thunbergii 124, 128-9, *128-9*
Pistacia (pistachio) *32-3*
  terebinthus 130-1, *130-1*
Podocarpus macrophyllus 132-3, *132-3*
pomegranate 7
powdery mildew 51, *51*
prices 18
privet, see *Ligustrum*
protection 26-7, *26*, *27*
pruning 57
  branches 43, *43*
  leaf 40-1
  regeneration 42, *42-3*
Prunus mume 39, 134-5, *134-5*
Pseudocydonia sinensis 136-7, *136-7*
Punica granatum (pomegranate) 7, 138-9, *138-9*
Pyracantha (firethorn) 140-1, *140-1*

Q

quince 44
  Chinese 136-7, *136-7*
  flowering 78-9, *78-9*

R

red spider mites 26
regeneration pruning 42, *42-3*
repotting 44, *45*
Rhododendron indica 142-3, *142*, *143*
root formation 16, *16*, *17*
root pruning 44, *45*

S

sacred bamboo 118-19, *118-19*
Sageretia theezans 144-5, *144-5*
sago palm 88
Salix (willow) 50
scale insects 51, 55, *55*
Serissa foetida 146-7, *146-7*
shade 22
shaping trees 33-47
  leaf pruning 40-1
  pruning branches 43, *43*
  regeneration pruning 42, *42-3*
  styles 34, *34-5*, *36-7*
  trimming 38, *38-9*
  with wire 17, 18, 46-7, *46-7*
soil 44, 57
Species Profiles 58-157
  key to 56-7
spider mites 26, 54
spruce, see *Picea*
Stewartia 15
  monadelpha 148-9, *148-9*
subtropical plants 15, *15*, 44
sunlight 22-4
suppliers 14-15, 158

T

Taxus:
  baccata (European) 150
  cuspidata (Japanese) 150-1, *150-1*

temperate plants 15
temperature 24-5, 57
temple juniper 104-5, *104-5*
theft 27
Tokonoma Bonsai Nursery 14
Tree of a thousand stars 146-7, *146-7*
trimming 38, *38-9*
tropical plants 14, 15, *15*, 44
trunk line 16-17, *16*, *17*

U

Ulmus (elm) 18
  parvifolia 152-3, *152*, *153*

V

vacation care 29
ventilation 26
vine weevils 52-3, *53*, 54, *54*

W

water, lime deposits from 25, *25*
watering 28-9, *28*, *29*, 57
willow 50
wind damage 24, 27
wiring 17, 18, 46-7, *46-7*
Wisteria 154-5, *154-5*

Y

yew, see *Taxus*
  plum-fruited/Chinese 132-3, *132-3*

Z

Zelkova serrata 156-7, *156-7*
Zen Buddhism 9

PHOTOGRAPHIC CREDITS

KEY: *a* above, *b* below

Dan Barton, 10, 23*b*, 24; Bonsai Centrum Heidelburg back cover (above centre), 58, 66, 76, 114*a*, 134*a*, 136, 138, 146; Martin Bradder 7; Craig Coussins 84; Suchin Ee front cover *b*, 94, 95; ET Archive 8; Federation of British Bonsai Societies 85; Paul Goff back cover (below right), 11*b*, 23*a*, 80, 92, 112*b*, 150; Kath Hughes 9, 85; Bill Jordan 50, 51, 52, 53, 106; Colin Lewis 9, 18, 46, 68, 112; Pius Notter 38, 39, 100, 101, 116; Walter Pall 11*b*, 106*a*, 114*b*, 122, 124, 134*b*; Harry Smith Horticultural Collection 78, 86, 104, 123, 144*b*; Peter Stiles 154*b*; Tokonama Bonsai Nursery 14.

All other photographs were taken at Lodder Vleuten BV, Utrechtseweg 21, 3451 GA Vleuten, Netherlands. We are grateful to both Mr G. Lodder and Kath Hughes for their kind interest and help with this book.

Every effort has been made to acknowledge copyright-holders, and Quarto would like to apologize if any omissions have been made.